Please Fall In Love With Me

(And Other High School Wishes)

Brandon Alvarado

To my middle school self, who would be proud to see me do something productive, or maybe embarrassed to see what I am writing.

Author's Note

The names I have included in this book, besides the names of immediate family members, have been changed to protect the identities of the people that are referenced in the essays. This does not affect the re-telling of events in the story.

Introduction

I have absolutely no business writing a book, and I am completely aware of that. I am from a generation that seems to be obsessed with putting it's every thought and action on social media for the world, and I am so entirely guilty of this by even writing this book.

This book was conceived in the form of a senior project at my high school, where any senior can work on a project based off of their passions and interests. Apparently, mine is talking about myself, and I am hoping that I am not a total narcissist. But, I have always wanted to write a book for two reasons: 1. Because it is super fucking cool to say that you wrote a book. 2. I was always looking for a book that could resemble my own life, my own feelings, my own fears, and my own ideas. Yes, you have your teen genre of books that have topics that range from horny vampires to sicknesses, but it can be tough to capture what the real teenage experience is like when an adult is the author of the book. Sure, they were also teenagers once, but I have not seen enough books that actual teenagers have written (fiction and non-fiction). So, I knew that I wanted to eventually write a book, but I did not know when I would do it. I especially did not think I was going to do it by the end of my senior year in high school. But, as cliché as this is, unexpected things can happen and life takes unexpected, and sometimes great, turns.

My experiences are absolutely not universal, and they are not supposed to be. I think many people forget that teenagers have their own experiences, and they are not all the teenagers you see in the movies that fill the bill of the horny and whiny side character to the stressed parents. These experiences are wholly my own, and I am excited to be able to share them with you.

I am not trying to start a revolution to change what the public thinks about teenagers. That would be very hard to do, and I can be very lazy. But, I am choosing to be honest about my own experiences by sharing my stories. I am choosing to keep it real at all times because I do not think I totally fit the bill of the many teenagers that are portrayed in movies.

So, my promise to you, reader, is that my stories are entirely true and have happened throughout my childhood, and many of these stories have shaped me to become who I am today. I hope you enjoy them, as I truly enjoyed writing them.

Xo,
Brandon

Diary-a

The Art of Word Vomiting in Many Childhood Journals

I had many childhood journals growing up, as I thought it would help me become more mature and wise in an age that is so immature. I bought my first journal in the fourth grade at the local Toy's "R" Us, a store I felt was the child equivalent to Macy's, and it was themed to one of the childhood films I used to always watch.

I bought the journal (AKA my parents bought the journal), and I immediately began writing when I took it home. I started writing about the food I was eating and the food I really wanted to eat instead. I wrote about the dreams I had about becoming someone that was noticed in a time that I realized childhood was the time period where you were noticed the most by the people around you. I wrote about the time I was supposed to go to sleep but secretly staying up instead to watch nothing but Nick at Nite. I wrote about the times my parents frustrated me because they did not take my fourth grade mind seriously. I wrote about the films and shows I watched and the films and shows I wanted to create. Even in the simplest and the most premature ways, I knew I had a story to tell, whether it was my own or a character's that I created.

As the next year went on, my journal was "lost" (I think my parents threw it in the trash thinking it was a raggedy coloring book), but the ideas stayed the same. I bought my next journal from the holiday sale my elementary school had every year before winter vacation. Students were encouraged to buy presents and trinkets for their family members at a price that was affordable for the everyday elementary school students (AKA how much money your parents were willing to cough up for presents for themselves). I didn't know that my parents would never use these presents, as I thought that a stuffed small baseball mitt with a team my parents do not like would be the best way to say "Merry Christmas!"

At this specific sale, I happen to have found one of the only items that had absolutely nothing to do with Christmas: a bright blue *American Idol* themed journal with a strange lock and key that looked like something Paula Abdul would create when doped up on medicine. I bought the journal, as well as some hideous earrings for my mother and mug for my father, and decided to change my journal-writing tactics: rather than write sporadically, I decided to write daily with a timestamp on top of the page. In the first week, I was able to keep up every day with my new goal. I once again wrote about the dinner I had and the secret snack I had after when no one was watching, the daily horrific soccer practice that my parents would make me attend rather than quit because they described my family as one that is filled with "try-ers and never quitters." I wrote about the daily trials and tribulations of being a fifth grader in a middle to upper class suburban community, which I can fully admit consists of not having enough cookies to feed the entire family dessert and not being able to watch my shows on TV because my family wanted to watch the new *American Idol* together on the couch.

"This is family time!" My mother would say as she was holding the two newest members of my five-person clan: my dog and a glass of fresh wine from the store.

While I was always in the mood to watch Mississippi residents try to sing "Oops I Did It Again" on the guitar on national television, my journal was calling for me to write more about the silly life I was leading as a fifth grader.

◆

When I was twelve years old, I decided to cleanse my room of anything from my "childhood" (as middle school kids describe their childhood consisting from birth to the ripe age of 10). I removed old books that screamed "CHILD!" to me, I put new books in the shelves that I was not really interested in reading but looked "adult" to me, and I found my old *American Idol* journal in one of the drawers on my nightstand. It was 2010, and the last time I wrote a journal entry was in 2008. The last entry I wrote about was how I was annoyed because my younger brother was hogging the Wii gaming system that my entire family enjoyed greatly. At this time, I still thought I would write every day, and then I just didn't. I do not remember exactly why I stopped writing in the journal. I tend to have big ideas about what I wanted to do, and then I would ignore them after a while. Part of me is surprised I kept writing in the journal that long before quitting, as my child brain was probably 10x worse at finishing a project than my late-teenage brain is now.

I read through some of the old posts in that journal, and I relished in the immature and, frankly, some of the ridiculous things I would think were real issues in my life. Even as a middle school kid, I was able to recognize this (although I would realize over the years that even the problems in middle school, while seemingly huge at the time, would mean nothing in my life years later). I read about the times where I was annoyed at my siblings or my parents for ludicrous reasons. I read about the times I wanted to become an actor, but I was too afraid to talk to some of my own classmates in the real world. I read about how I wished I were smarter than I was, and I read about how I was excited to no longer be treated like a kid when I entered middle school.

I threw away my *American Idol* journal in the seventh grade, and I began a new one that year with a *Twilight* theme. During this time, the *Twilight* hype was at its highest peak, where middle school kids dreamed that they were the Bella looking for their Edward in a place where the real boys lacked deodorant and thought that the word "feminist" was probably a synonym for "very gay" (I am sure many still believe that now). The hype was not lost upon me, and I bought a four-pack *Twilight* journal collection with each journal following the theme of each book/film. It was a ridiculous purchase, but I thought I would write in all of those journals. When I got home, I took out the first one (themed to the first book, of course) and began writing the date and time on the top of the page. It all came back to me then, the idea of writing every day and keeping this daily journal that would contain my deepest thoughts that I could look back on when I was leading a better adult life.

Rather than writing about my young elementary school years, I wrote about my uncomfortable middle school years. Rather than writing about how I was annoyed with my brother and sister, I wrote about how my friends did not want to be friends with me anymore. I wrote about how I tried desperately hard to get them back. I wrote about my desperations to still not be looked at as a kid. I wrote about my confused sexuality. I wrote about how I didn't like going to church and I didn't know why. I wrote about my dreams and aspirations of leaving a town as small as mine and making a name for myself in a world like this one.

I recently thought about my reasons for writing in these journals. I realized that, even as a young child, I thought that I could look back on these journals during a simpler time before I became someone "big" in the world, whether that would actually happen or not. I thought I had a story to tell, whether it was talking about the food I ate for dinner or if it was talking about the mean name someone called me before school started for the day. I didn't know who would see it, as there were parts of me that both wanted people to see it and never wanted people to even look at the cover. I finished writing in the *Twilight* journal about a year after I started writing in it, and I didn't write in a journal consistently after that. Instead, I wrote little posts when I would feel sad and feel like I needed vent without actually having to talk to a human being. While not writing in a journal after middle school, I did have the chance to reflect on why I started writing in the first place, and I thought about why I continue writing now.

There is a comfort in word vomiting on to the page. There is a feeling I get when putting words down on to the pages. I am not sure if it is the documentation of my thoughts that make my thoughts and emotions feel more legitimate to me. Although I haven't kept up with it consistently, I never let the idea of writing my feelings leave my life, whether it was writing on paper for myself or writing something to be read in front of an audience. No matter what, I have accepted the idea that I can never let writing and "journaling" out of my life, nor do I want to.

As you can see, I am doing it now.

Brandon Clinton, Presidential Candidate: The Time I Thought of Myself as a Liberal Middle School Kid

I was not one of those people who recognized how terrible middle school was when I was younger. No. I recognized how terrible it was when I while I was still attending middle school. I was shocked at my brother's graduation when one of the student speakers described middle school as "the best time of my life!" I'm sure he just didn't realize how much better it would get once he graduated, but middle school should never be the peak of your life. Ever.

While in middle school, I once thought of myself as someone who could qualify as the most progressive student they have ever seen in their life. I had absolutely no reasons to qualify for this title, as the most liberal thing I did was cry in public when someone was making fun of me at recess. But, I do remember one day where I felt that I took the cake as the most liberal middle school kid that ever stepped foot on the blacktop with pride the size of my oversized jeans my parents made me wear (as they thought I would eventually grow into them).

It was Halloween 2009. It's a day I don't like to remember very often. It's a day that I have to almost leave the room when my friends discuss it. During this time, my favorite show was *Ugly Betty*, an American version of a former Spanish telenovela. The story was about a girl, an "ugly duckling" if you will, who begins working at a fashion magazine. I thought it was the "coolest" thing I have ever seen. I thought she represented myself and every other middle school kid who felt uncomfortable and strange, which is mostly everyone besides a select few. She walked into the office for the first time with her glasses, braces, and a Guadalajara poncho that Joan Rivers would have completely ripped apart in an episode of *Fashion Police* without missing a single beat.

Thinking I could be the most progressive middle school kid, my twelve year old self decided to dress up as the title character, Betty Suarez, for Halloween that year and wear it all day in school. My parents did not stop this decision, which I wonder to this day is because I might have done something wrong and this was a punishment without the official ruling. Instead, they drove me to the store to buy this costume. I did notice a look in my father's eyes that wanted to stop the horror of what was to come, but that didn't stop him from letting my pick out the rattiest wig in the bunch that could be found. I already had part of the costume, as I was already sporting the clear braces, which was as commonly worn in middle school as underwear, and I bought the poncho and the glasses that could complete the costume. Luckily, the poncho and glasses came together in a special package that was from the actual show itself because the poncho itself would probably only be found in the real Guadalajara, Mexico on the sidewalk next to the local convenience store.

On the actual holiday, I excitedly put on my outfit while my mother gave me her lipstick to put on. By the time I was ready for school, I looked like a cross between a *RuPaul's Drag Race* reject, a hooker on the side of an old city road (without the fishnets and boots to go along with it, as I learned by watching *Pretty Woman*), and a wife/mother that was just arrested for domestic assault and possession of crack cocaine. The poncho itself would have had me beaten up in the real Guadalajara, Mexico, and the red lipstick made me looked like someone punched me in the mouth and I just did not clean it up.

"How do I look, mom?" My idiotic twelve-year-old self asked my mother.

My mother made a face like she just received notice that there was a recall for the anti-aging creams she uses, and instead they would make her look older.

"You look great! Everyone is going to love it!"

In her mind, she was concerned that my look was so bad that it was going to peel the school walls and she would have to pay for the renovations.

Pre-iPhone selfie culture, I ran to my bedroom to find my large digital camera that my parents let me keep after buying a new one. I ran back into the bathroom, made sure my lipstick was in place, and took the most ridiculous selfie that would have made Kim Kardashian have an aneurysm.

My mother dropped me off at school that day, and my frizzy wig entered the back of the school five minutes before the rest of my body does. When I finally make it to the spot that my friends and I usually stand, I waited alone while waiting for my other friends to arrive in their normal costumes. Standing alone, I resembled a lonely Mexican prostitute with the messy wig a tourist with the Guadalajara poncho that someone would buy thinking that's what "the 'people' wear here." I would like to think of myself as someone who is running for an election at this time. I was putting myself out there and beginning my campaign as the most liberal middle school kid (this was before I became an atheist). It was looking like my campaign symbol was a messy black wig that resembled a used mop.

As I waited in all of my lipstick and no-shame-filled glory, I heard the voices of my political opponents in the form of pre-teen boys hollering behind me. Not only were groups split up based on their class, groups within each class were split up as well. The pre-teen girls, where I was the only the boy in the group, stood towards the back field while many of the pre-teen boys stood towards the door where everyone would walk into right before class started. As I stood alone, I hear the boys calling the name of someone that is actually in my group of friends.

"Ana!" They shouted. "Ana, is that you?"

The only problem was that person was not actually there. Instead, they thought I, wearing the hideous poncho, glasses, and a messy wig, was that person.

I stood in silence hoping their curiosity would die down.

"Ana!" The shouting continued, and I wanted to cave in the poncho.

Still thinking they would stop, I stood in silence with my back turned to them. Instead, the boys left their nest and walked over to find that who they thought was Ana was actually a pre-teen boy with too much lipstick on.

"…Oh," they said as they watched me in confusion.

All I could mutter was a "hello" to them as I stood there hoping there wasn't any food from breakfast in the wig.

"Sorry, we thought you were Ana…" they muttered right before they retreated back to their home base.

What was funny to me was that, even if Ana was standing alone, what caused them to walk over in the first place? On any normal day, they would have kept to themselves by the door and not have even noticed our group walk by. But today, they decided they would walk over to see who they thought was Ana in the flesh. Was it the foreign-looking poncho? Was it the glasses that were made from plastic and could have easily been broken if I grabbed them a little too tight? Was it the wig that made me look like I had a rough night with Christian Grey? Was it the fact that I didn't turn around when they hollering to me?

Whatever it was, this was the day they decided to come over, and I didn't think much of it once the day actually began. Instead, I basked in the glory of what I thought I achieved at the age of 12: tolerance that I felt was lacking in middle school due to the ignorance of people ages 10-12. But, even I was ignorant about many things. I didn't really know what the word "transgender" meant that well. I knew the basics of the term, but I didn't know the real struggle transgender youth go through on a daily basis. To this day, I don't know the half of what they go through because I have not experienced what they experienced. I know a lot more about it now as I have grown a little older, but at the time I did really know what I was doing. What I thought was a "political" move was really an idea that wrapped around the child-like innocence that comes in the form of dressing up for Halloween. I was always fascinated with living the life of someone else, as I was never really comfortable with the life I was living as a middle school kid. I was not at all comfortable with myself, and I thought playing dress-up would be a fun way to live the life of someone else for a change. But, the idea went from imagining a different life to walking into school with a wiry black wig and still feeling uncomfortable in the skin I chose to wear that day.

Ultimately, this led me to wrap up my childhood fantasies in a blanket that yelled "politics!" and "change!" I didn't think it was a problem I had with myself. Rather, I thought the problems I had could be solved if I blamed the problem on everyone else and then proceed to fix it. Thus, I wanted to become that "liberal middle school" kid. At the same time, I felt that I had no other choice but to take a title like that. I only hung out with girls, the sound of my voice made some people uncomfortable, and I showed up to school dressed in *Ugly Betty* drag. The problem was really that I did not accept myself, but I did not understand that until now. So at that time, I still thought I could be the "liberal middle school kid" that I thought I was destined to be.

◆

I was sitting on my bed when I received a phone call from one of my best friends (and the leader of my group). In the group, there were just three girls and me being the only boy. One of the three girls was seen as sort of a leader of the pack, but we didn't really see that at the time. She called me up on a random Friday afternoon, and we had just seen each other in school only hours earlier.

"We are not friends anymore. Don't ever talk to me again. Don't call me or text me, and don't speak to me at school," She growled. The phone call was very muffled, as if she was walking with a giant crowd as she was speaking.

"What are you talking about?"

"Don't ever speak to me again. Leave me alone."

Before I could even respond, she hung up the phone. She was like a small dog that bites you and runs away. Not getting the message clear enough, I called her back.

"Are you not understanding me? Leave me alone! Don't call me again. I hate you!" she barked, and then she hangs up the phone again.

I put the phone down in shock, and I don't know how to react. I want to talk to her, but she refuses to let me get a word in edgewise. I have no idea what I did, as we shared a peanut butter and jelly sandwich in school earlier that day. I thought about anything I could have possibly done to receive a phone call so vicious. I didn't get up from my bed, as I receive the next phone call from friend #2.

"Hello?" I mutter.

"Don't ever talk to me again. We are not friends anymore, and I never want to see you again."

The phone is hung up before I can take a breath.

Like clockwork, I receive notification from friend #3. This time, it was in the form of a text message, as if I already taken enough bullets from this drive-by shooting.

The message reads: We can't be friends anyone. Please don't talk to me anymore.

Boom, three shots and I am down. At that point, I realized that I heard the muffles coming from friend #1's phone because the three of them were together when they did that. I continued to sit on my bed and wait for a response, but I knew there isn't one coming. I am not sure what exactly happened, but being too impatient to take a breath, I tried calling them while hysterically crying. You would have thought I lost a close family member from the way I was crying, as middle school always calls for being overly dramatic and a little awkwardly sweaty. None of the three Heathers picked up the phone, and I spent my weekend wondering what had happened and what I did to cause this. I was confused, desperate, disheveled, and in need of a glass of apple juice and a bowl of chips immediately. Feeling very adult-like, my mother let me drink apple juice out of wine glass as I expressed my confusion and sadness over the situation.

That Monday, I walked in to school thinking things might have been smoothed over. Although we didn't speak over the weekend, my naïve mind wanted me to believe that they would tell me what they did was a silly prank and didn't mean anything. Instead, they walked past me with their attitudes icier than a Snowmaggedon. I was losing my support system for my candidacy for the most liberal middle school kid. But more importantly, I was losing my best friends that I trusted. My mom always warned me about putting too many eggs in one basket, as I have had a few very close friends in my childhood that I have lost and it's never really easy to move on. I was guilty of doing this now. These were the people I trusted and relied on in ways I wouldn't do the same with the just casual acquaintances, and it was the first day in a long time I felt like I had no one on my side.

I remember walking into the cafeteria that day for lunch, and I sat down at their table because I didn't feel like I had anywhere to sit (did I mention I didn't have much respect for myself in middle school?). Immediately, the head of the group turned to me while the other two sat in silence swallowing both their sandwiches and the tension that was created.

"What are you doing at this table?" snarled the HBIC (Head B In Charge- I didn't curse much in middle school).

"I don't have anywhere else to sit."

"Well, you can't sit here!"

In typical middle school dramatic fashion, I jumped up from the table in tears and ran to the bathroom to have an old-fashioned cry session with a piece of toilet paper. The girls did not react to my crying, and I specifically remember the HBIC yelling at me as I left the room. It was one of the many times in my post-elementary school career that I felt like I was in a movie moment. All that was needed to make it complete was for someone to follow me in the bathroom and tell me that I didn't need those people in my life while giving me an extra piece of toilet paper and letting me share their snack their mother packed for them. But, in the real world, I was alone in the bathroom for five minutes while life continued on the cafeteria. At one point, someone came in to pee and then proceeded to shuffle by me to wash their hands.

I began to channel *Mean Girls* while making friends with the bathroom sink. Besides the fact that I began watching that movie at a very inappropriate age (I saw it for the first time at the age of seven, just so you know) so I knew too much about it already, I didn't want to be Lindsay Lohan sitting on the toilet seat eating her sandwich alone. I was running a campaign in my mind to become the most liberal middle school kid, and this campaign did not involve sitting in the bathroom stall on my own. I decided to leave the bathroom and continue my lonesome crusade, but I first had to make my face stop looking like it was trying to match the shade of a ripe tomato. After the extra three minutes or so in the bathroom, I walked out of the bathroom and back to the same table that kicked me out.

"What are you doing back here? I told you couldn't sit here!" HBIC yelled.

"I have no where else to sit so leave me alone! I just wont talk to you guys then!"

I quietly ate my sandwich and snack and waited for the lunch period to be over. It was one of the more humiliating experiences of my middle school years, and I couldn't believe I went back to sit with them. Forgetting the political crusade that I created in my own mind, my self-respect was completely out the window the moment I planted myself in that seat. What I thought was a brave move in the moment turned out to be one that was pathetic and desperate, and soon the toilet seemed like it was calling as a new place to eat my lunch.

◆

A few weeks passed by, and the campaign against me was running strong. Only, the ones against me were the ones I thought were on my side the entire time. One Friday night, the school was hosting one of its monthly "Teen Scene" events in the cafeteria. These events were meant to bring students together to do activities that were extremely age appropriate, like ice skating and dancing to Katy Perry songs in the gymnasium. Anything that may look like grinding, even the accidental butt touch when you walk past someone (I have had many of those), the teachers that were begrudgingly chaperoning the event would walk over and put an end to it before your private region could even figure out what was happening.

For whatever reason that possessed me to do this, I decided to attend the event and I enter the scene "solo" with a sprinkle of hope dusted in my dirty sneakers. When running for the candidacy of most liberal kid, I could not miss an event like this. Can you imagine the President missing one of his many White House parties? This was basically the same thing except I was not actually running for anything, nor was I important enough in the school community to be even considered the assistant to a Congressman, and the White House equated to the middle school gymnasium and cafeteria that smelled like sweat and puberty at its peak. But, these little details were absolutely not stopping me from thinking highly of myself, as kids tend to think the world revolves around their pubescent world.

I pick up my already sweaty feet and walk into the cafeteria with my pride in one hand and my flip phone in the other, as I waited for a text from anyone in the room that may say, "Hey come here! Let's hang out together!" Ten minutes later, I never received that text, so I spent the time picking up a soda and pretending to text other people. As a "candidate," I had to always look busy for the crowd. If there wasn't a person (probably not even an acquaintance of mine) to say hi to, there was always a fake person to text to pass the time.

Another ten minutes after that, the girls, led by HBIC, walked into the cafeteria with every middle school girl's nightclub outfit: a t-shirt with a disenchanting design and slogan on it with black leggings and boots with a small heel. I had no place to comment on clothes, as I was wearing my dad's sweatshirt with a questionable stain on it as well as jeans that didn't fit me and sneakers that were in the beginning stages of becoming just a sole. I watched as the girls walk right past me and towards the gymnasium with posture that made them look like they were being carried by a puppeteer and looks on their faces as if they had sticks shoved up their reers.

I walked towards the gymnasium around a minute after they headed over. This time, I was not looking for forgiveness for whatever I did to them (at this time, I still had no idea). Instead, I was looking to confront HBIC about what was going on. Even I, a known pushover, was reaching my limit. It had been too long, and I still did not know what I did to hurt them so badly, as they told me it was "none of my business." But, the hurt was growing too large, and I knew I had to confront the group in person because they wouldn't answer my phone calls.

I walked into the gym with energy and passion that I assume came from the pizza rolls my mother fed me right before I left. I found the girls standing in the midst of the other standing students, as the music was playing but the "dancing" (meaning moving your body up and down until someone started actually doing a legit dance move), and I trudge over to the group.

"I am sick of this! What have I done to deserve this kind of treatment?" I asked in the same tone one would use if they were getting arrested for DUI.

"None of your business!" HBIC barked at me as if I asked her when the last time she defecated (or middle school lingo- "number two").

They all walked away together, and they seem to share the same attitude as they leave the gymnasium, until one of them accidentally tripped on their own growing feet. They ignored this and continue walking.

I, not having enough of humiliating myself and also not satisfied, followed them back to the cafeteria for round two.

"You can't just walk away from me like that!"

"I just did!"

"We were best friends, and you are acting like you have never met me before!"

"We are not friends!"

26

Round two ended with the girls, led by HBIC, picking up sodas from the other side of cafeteria. While, HBIC had the support of the two other friends, the empty chair by the wall led my support team as well as the actual wall itself. I knew I wasn't going to win this fight, and I knew I wasn't going to get an answer out of HBIC. The thing I learned about HBIC after our friendship ended was that she was only powerful with a group of people around her. Without the group surrounding her, she was completely powerless. She was only quick with responses because the other people around her were fueling her. When she was alone, she was just as vulnerable as I was. I began to realize this as this verbal fight continued, and I sat down to lick my wounds knowing that HBIC would win unless she was really taken out of her element.

What surprised me the most out of all the things HBIC has ever said happened once I sat down to end verbal boxing match. Out of the corner of my eye, I watched HBIC and company walk towards me, and I prepared myself for what might come next. I tried to think of things to say in case she started up again. From the look on her face, which looked like a face you would make if someone took your iPhone and throw it on the ground, she was preparing herself for round three. I reminded myself that I am prepared and I can handle whatever is coming my way, and it looked like the Rottweiler was making her way over to her vicious chew toy.

Without a beat, she yelled "Why don't you just tell everyone you're gay!"

Whatever I thought of in my mind completely escaped me in that one moment. I was shocked that she took it that far, and I didn't know what to say. It was a low blow to make, and it felt like she took my pants off in front of everyone. At the time, I was questioning my own sexuality, and I was completely unsure of myself. Really, I knew who I was, but I didn't want to acknowledge nor accept it yet. But, she hit the Achilles heal with perfect aim. What was the most disappointing part was not even that she pointed this out to everyone around us, but she tried to use my own sexuality as an insult.

Round three ended before it ever really started, and I was knocked out, and my candidacy for the most liberal middle school kid was over. Looking back on this time now, I realize that I never really had the title in the first place, as much as I thought I did. I was not at all comfortable with myself, and I couldn't even come out to myself before someone like HBIC confronted me about it. I couldn't expect other people to accept me if I didn't yet accept myself. This may sound preachy, but this is something I find to be so true to this day. I couldn't blame other people for not being tolerant or accepting when I was not accepting of myself. My self-respect was still hiding in the closet, even when HBIC tried to push me out of it.

◆

A few months after the fight originally began, I received a gmail chat (the 2009 version of IMing) from HBIC, saying she forgave me for what I "did to her." Like clockwork, I received a message from both friend #1 and friend #2 with their letter of forgiveness. Even at the time, I was lonely and desperate, and I took them back with open arms. It wasn't until a year after HBIC and company forgave me that I finally confronted HBIC at the most inappropriate time about the silliest thing with the passion and resentment I still had from the year prior. While I was out of the closet to my friends at that time, my self-respect did not journey into the bright world for a while after that.. If I had the slightest bit of respect for myself, I know things would have ended up differently.

On another note, after the fight ended, I eventually learned what caused HBIC to hate me, and I learned that it was because she felt I was annoying and felt that I spoke too close to people's faces, which sounds like the best and worst Congressional candidate to me.

Coming Out and Going In

Not too many people went to the library after school back in the day, but it was always the same crowd. Usually, the people that were there had to wait for their parents to pick them up since many of them were working and could not make it on time. Being that both my parents worked, I waited at the library for my babysitter to pick me up. But, I never minded because I would sit with my friends, and oddly, there was more "drama" (AKA middle school drama) in one of the quietest places (theoretically) you could be at rather than a place where it was loud so no one could hear you ramble about not getting the new iPhone and hating your parents for it (like maybe the schoolyard?).

Being a dramatic child, I planned to come out to my friends in a way that seemed to fit my personality. So naturally, rather than come out in total privacy, I decided to come out to my best friend behind the shelves of the town library, as I didn't think about how completely shady that would look to anyone else.

I remember the day I planned to come out to Tyler. At the time, we were not as close as we are now, but I always knew I could trust her. Tyler is one of those people that can keep any secret and still keep the best compassionate face and always have the best response. I could tell her one day that I murdered my parents in an angry fit for the most ridiculous reason (ex. they finished my leftover food, they told me that my shirt didn't fit me right, they came into my room when I was sleeping, they said "hello" to me at just the wrong time), and I know she would not say a single word to anyone else and she would act like my murder was perfectly reasonable to keep both of our sanities.

I knew I wanted to come out after having my first crush on a guy in seventh grade. What turned from an in-my-mind epic-love story between him and another girl in my class that kept me occupied when I was bored turned into me realizing that I actually wanted to be part of that love story and I wanted the girl to officiate our wedding instead. Perfectly natural progression, I know. But I thought of my friends having big mouths, and I was worried about being judged. I knew one friend that would tell another friend that was a homophobe due to her religious upbringing. I knew another friend that I thought would tell the other friend that would tell the homophobe because I thought the second girl could guilt the original girl into telling her my "secret." So, I knew that one of the only people I could share my true thoughts with at the time was Tyler.

We sat in English class in our eighth grade year, and while someone in the class was reading "Wherefore art though, Romeo?" like she was being stabbed in the stomach but was oddly alright with it, I mouthed to Tyler that I wanted her to join me in the library after school. She usually didn't go to the library, but I was able to convince her to come with me. My heart was racing, and I couldn't continue paying attention to *Romeo and Juliet* any longer. 1. I had no idea what they were saying. 2. I was about to share something to someone else that I literally just acknowledged about myself only around a week ago. I mean, I remember being attracted to boys as a kid, but I never really came to terms with what it actually was until that eighth grade year.

After school, Tyler and I walked to library, and rightfully so, she keept questioning me about why we were going and what she had to tell me. Me, still being dramatic, acted like it was a dramatic cliffhanger in a soap opera and she would just have to wait until the next episode to see what was to happen.

"You have to wait until we get to the library!" I said as the dramatic music in my head played at its highest volume.

We walk into the library, where the librarians look like they have seen a rat infestation every day when the middle school kids come in. I look around to see an aisle where there would be no librarian stacking books, and I took Tyler to one of the farthest ones away from where the other middle school kids sat after school. Besides that, someone (a friend of a friend, you know how it is in middle school) was asking what was going on, and it was more dramatic to try and whisk off in a library rather than to just tell her to leave us alone. As one might say, it was the "gayer" thing to do, and I am just representing the LGBT community the right way.

In the middle of the aisle, on a random weekday, I came out to the girl who is now my best friend. Of course, I started crying, and it was a moment that would have been reality TV gold, and the girl that kept asking what was going on might has well been the cameraman for the project. Tyler, being extremely open and liberal and possibly relishing in the idea of being a gay icon at the age of thirteen, was completely supportive and wonderful throughout the whole thing, which was the reaction I think I needed at the time. After I came out to her, our status of best friendship really began, and for years to come it would consist of fake-apartment shopping (looking at towels and candles at Kmart, which would make our parents totally proud) and being referred to as the new Will and Grace by my mother.

◆

I came out to my mother in the summer of 2011, right before my freshman year of high school began. She was cooking dinner and on the phone with my grandparents, and I was hyped up after the very recent release of Lady GaGa's "Born This Way." A couple of nights before, my mother and I were watching an episode of *Glee* (back when we actually sat down to watch *Glee*) and she saw two male characters kissing on screen. This led to a debate on whether gay characters should be seen being affectionate on network television, and I was offended that she felt it should not be shown on network television where "anyone" can turn the channel on and watch. Generally, I hate the argument where people act like gay people kissing is equal to watching soft-core porn on cable channels. We would never say something like that about straight couples sharing a kiss on network television because that is seen as the "natural" way. I have seen politicians make comments all the time about same-sex relationships, as heterosexual congressmen are the ones that seem to be making the decisions on the rights of LGBT people. But, it was different with my mother, and it was a lot more personal than just watching this on television.

Due to my mother's expression of her beliefs (which have changed over the years), I felt that it was time to tell her the truth about my own sexuality. At the same time, I thought it would heal me a bit from my own insecurities, as the weight would be lifted from my shoulders. Her attention was focused on the chicken she was cooking, and then she let it burn as she cried to me. She was happy that I told her the truth, but she was worried and scared about my future. She felt that life would be "harder" for me because of my sexuality. I told my father a little while later, after he got home from work, and he immediately took a couple of shots and tried to kindly ask if it was a phase without making it sound like I was going through a major rebellious phase.

"Mom! Dad! I hate you both so I like penis now! Surprise! Do we have any more milk in the fridge or should I have my older male black lover get it? Oh yeah, that's another surprise."

When I told him it wasn't a phase, he took one more shot for safety, and I thought about the possibility of joining him with a shot of bleach topped with some laundry detergent.

I came out to my brother three years later at a burger place, where I would have immediately ordered a hot dog for a subliminal message if they were selling it. Instead, I told him after I took a long sip of soda through a large straw. Months after that, I told my sister in the car after she thought Bruno Mars was gay and apparently I had to show her what a real gay male looked like. She said she already knew, which didn't help my case, and it was the typical response I received from people that I have told.

It wasn't that my parents were ashamed of my sexuality, but they were worried about how people in town would take it if I were open about it. Thus, I was not encouraged to "spread it around" because my personal life was "private" (you can see I totally took this advice by writing this book). But, I didn't mind this the first year after I told my friends and family. Coming out for the first few times felt like getting teeth pulled while high on laughing gas: the high was so great that you couldn't always feel the pain. Once the laughing gas wore off, I began to feel the pain and the self-hatred that I thought I would avoid when I first told Tyler in the library. The self-hatred came slowly and began to pile up as time went on, and it really began my freshman year of high school. Before I knew it, I was lost in a cloud of my own insecurities and I couldn't find my way out of it.

◆

Tyler and I had a very good friend in middle school, and I will call her D. Tyler was friends with her before I was, but I had some memories of her before we became close. She was bright, excited, and happy most of the time, which can be almost impossible in middle school. She liked to read and write, and she liked to play music. I don't remember the exact moment Tyler and I realized something was off because things were beginning to change in stages. It was not a situation where one specific thing happened and that caused a major change. Rather, the change was happening the same time I became closer and closer with her.

When freshman year began, she and I both had biology together. Being in a class with her every day, I was able to see a change in her behavior gradually. Her attitude changed, and she was acting different than she did only a year ago. At the time, I didn't think too much about it because I was wrapped up in my own inner turmoil, as I had the same disease many other teenagers had: thinking the world revolved around me when it absolutely did not. No one cared that I cried over silly things, and I didn't always notice when one of my close friends was going through a depression that would only get deeper as the year went on. Besides that, Tyler and I could not do much because we didn't know the half of what was really going on until we suddenly did.

For over a year, we would receive pictures of cuts D would give herself using items such as staples and razor blades. There would be cuts on her arms and legs, and she would try and keep them on her legs rather than her arms because cuts on legs can be hidden more easily than cuts on arms. One picture a week turned into two pictures a week and then sometimes turned into three pictures a week, and I was watching a friend go on a complete downward spiral without knowing what to do. Tyler and I were fourteen years old, and we were not even qualified to study a paper cut.

D eventually went to treatment after her parents decided to try and control the situation, and she checked out not too long after she checked in. For a while, we thought it might have been over, and I don't blame that on a fourteen-year-old naivety, as I believe that anyone of any age would hope that a rehab stint would help their friend stop harming him or herself. Nevertheless, the cutting resumed, and it was documented with every picture that was sent to Tyler and I. For a while, we felt powerless. How are we supposed to control a situation that doesn't even seem to be able to be controlled by doctors? This was where the naivety of a fourteen-year-old freshman in high school came in. A person cannot be magically cured, as much as you want them to be. A person cannot be helped unless they wanted to get help themselves. D did not want help, and Tyler and myself, nor could her parents or doctors, force her to want to change and recover. Instead, Tyler and I had to watch, but we became frustrated by the lack of help. While we felt her parents were not doing enough to control what was going on, we were the ones receiving the photos of lines of blood and cuts that were created roughly twenty minutes before the photos were sent. Her parents may not have seen as much as we saw, even though they were living with her. Or maybe they did, and they didn't want to admit there was a real issue going on. I will never know the answer to that, nor is it really my business. In the simplest of terms, it can be like a parents having to talk to a teacher that is accusing their child of bullying another kid. There is a defense wall that goes up because there is a need for many parents to protect their children, and I do not have to be a parent to notice this.

I can remember the last day I saw D before she went to rehab for a longer period of time for extended treatment. Tyler and I made frequent trips to D's house to both hang out with her, as she was no longer going to the same high school as we were, and to check to see how she was doing. The day we went over her house, she was showing us where she was hiding the staples she used to cut herself. She showed us the CD player where she would hide the staples and some razor blades. She showed us the cabinet in the bathroom where she would hide them. She took us to the "secret spot," a woodsy area near her house that overlooked a reservoir, where she was sharpening her blades and attempting to take a set of blades from a pencil sharpener from her house. What was scary about the whole situation was no longer the fact that she was cutting herself (that statement itself is very telling of how far it got with D and how severe the situation was), but it was scary that there was no longer a distance between Tyler, myself, and the blades. When we received the pictures, D already made the cuts on her skin. The sharpening of the blades happened in privacy, and the cuts happened in privacy. Now, she was cutting her blades in front of us. The distance was gone, and Tyler and I didn't know how to handle the situation in the moment. Oddly, we tried to act normally throughout the whole day because we didn't want to cause a commotion with D, as she was alarmingly fragile. We tried to do normal activities that fourteen year olds would do, like take photos by the reservoir or watch a movie. D couldn't take the photos with us because she was too busy sharpening the blade she got from the pencil sharpener after smashing it against a rock. D couldn't watch a movie because she was too busy cutting her legs in her bathroom with the freshly sharpened razor. Tyler and I went home that day knowing that something had to be done, but the worst didn't come yet.

The text I received from D one day was not a picture of cuts, nor was it a text talking about she just hurt herself. Instead, it was a cryptic goodbye note that ended with "I'm sorry." Tyler came over my house, and to this day, it was one of the only times I've ever seen Tyler cry. We tell our parents, and we call the police. From what I understand, the police found D in the bathroom about to hang herself, and she was immediately taken in for treatment.

While she was in rehab, Tyler and I would receive phone calls from her on a weekly basis. We were never able to call her, but we had to wait until she called both of us in a two-way phone call. Usually, the phone calls would consist of casual conversation, or the most casual conversation you could have when one party is in a mental facility.

"How's school?" She would ask us.

"It's ok," I would respond. "Is the food good there?"

We tried our best to keep it as normal as possible, as not only it was new for D, but also Tyler and I were not doctors that dealt with these types of situations every day. I always thought from the movies I would watch that teenagers screamed in their pillow when they were upset. Hiding the blades that you used to cut yourself was foreign territory for me, and thousands of school presentations of the dangers of self-harm could not prepare someone for what really happens until they witness it themselves.

While the phone calls usually were not too heavy (considering the situation), Tyler and I were trying to be hopeful, as we couldn't expect anything. Unfortunately, the phone calls were no longer friendly conversation. Rather, D told us how much she hated us for what we did, and she wouldn't ever forgive us. There was a front that Tyler and I tried to keep up, as we felt there was no other choice. We had to be strong and take the heat with the hopes that she would one day change her mind. I later, years later, realized that her reaction was not irrational because she still didn't want to change for the better. She was not ready to recover because she was thrown into this world where she was totally uncomfortable. She was taken into treatment because we called the police that day. There was a point, despite her hatred for us at the time, Tyler and I had to remind ourselves that we did what we had to do as friends. If we didn't call the police, we would have never seen D again. Even if she hated us, hearing her voice was easier to handle than no longer hearing her say anything again because we didn't take her threat seriously and call the police.

Eventually, D was released from rehab again, and she thanked us for helping her when she needed it. We didn't expect, nor truly want a thank you from D. We did what we thought was the right thing to do. Not even as friends, but it was the right thing to do for anyone that might have known her, or at least received the text messages. The house visits were no longer serving the purpose of seeing how she might have harmed herself, but it was to really hang out the way freshmen and sophomores in high school do: watch movies, take photos. It was the same as what we did before, but this time she was in the photo with us.

◆

D was thrown into a situation she was not comfortable with, but I was not. I willingly came out to my family and friends, but we both did not know how to deal with the consequences of our actions. While D lashed out on Tyler and I, I lashed out at my own friends. I acted like they weren't there for me when they were. I thought I didn't fit in, and for a while, I thought something was wrong with me. Looking back, I realized how much self-hatred I had for myself when D was going through everything too, but we just reacted to our own self-hatred differently. D was cutting herself and trying to feel something during the times she didn't feel anything at all, as she was suffering from a mental disease. I did not harm myself physically, but I was harming myself emotionally by feeling everything: happiness, sadness, pain, joy, excitement, and hatred. I was excited to finally be out of the closet with the ones I love, and I was hopeful for the things to come, but I wasn't truly able to accept or love myself at the same time. I wanted to feel everything that I thought I was supposed to feel when you are out of the closet, but I never turned to a razor blade to find it.

I watched D fall apart at the same time I was falling apart, but our reasons for doing so were different. Our outcomes were similar, but I just didn't have the scars to prove my damaged emotional state. But, I always knew D was suffering more than I would ever begin to understand, which is why our situations are only minimally comparable when you think about it. I was suffering because of my experiences and trying to understand society's view of people like me. D was suffering from a mental disease that she could not control herself. I am lucky because my own emotional pain is one that can be controlled by myself due to my own view of the world around me.

As I sat down to write this piece, I thought to myself about the pain we all suffer through, whether that is proven through rehab stints or just emotional crying in my bed while on the phone with my friend (freshman year was not a pretty time for Brandon). No matter what our experiences are, and no matter what background we have, we are all suffering from something in some way. We all have pain that we hide, and even the happiest of people on the outside are struggling with their own demons. The difference between one person's situation and another's is how they react to what they are going through. We can either accept our surroundings, and ourselves or we can want to destroy ourselves little by little and let our surroundings completely control the way we live our lives. D went through so much pain in the past, and I will never forget the moments I shared with her as I watched her fall downward in her own mental state, but I also watched D eventually rise up again and see her truly smile once again. The same happened with myself, as I once again began to smile and grow more confidence than I ever had in my life before. But our pain was dealt with differently, as I turned to my family and friends for help and eventually had to rely on myself to finally accept the person I am. For others, like D, they need help from other resources, like doctors, because it is harder, and sometimes impossible, to change their own view by themselves.

I know now that we all suffer from some sort of pain in some way, but the way it is dealt with is the defining wall that splits up someone that is considered "crazy" and someone who is considered "not crazy" because the former had to go to treatment. In reality, for many people, "crazy" isn't the term used to describe someone who went to treatment. We use these terms because there are people too afraid to admit that they are suffering emotionally, and they feel the need to throw labels like that to gratify their own struggles. If there is anything I learned about watching D and looking at my own experiences, it is that we both were suffering, but only one of us visited a rehab center for treatment because they needed help because their treatment was out of their control, but she was never "crazy" in the way many people would describe her. She was a bright and happy fifth grade girl, who I would see at the town's events, and I watched her become a depressed teenager that needed help but didn't where to turn to, but she eventually found her way out the other side. There was a little fifth grade boy, who was happy and bright, and he became a teenager that hated himself and didn't know where to always turn to, but he found his way out the other side. A label split the two, as one was diagnosed with depression, but they both grew with the support of friends and family and, as many others do, one just needed another resource to rely on for help.

My Brother and I:

How Kyle and I Don't Understand How We Are Related

I was born in 1997, and my brother was born in 1999. As children, we would always play together, and we would take the cars our parents and relative bought us and roll them around the house for hours. We were entertained by watching movies relating to racecars (and we both enjoyed *Mean Girls* at a scary age). As we got older, my parents began to notice more of the differences between myself and my brother, and now sometimes I'm surprised we like so many of the same things when we were younger, but then I remember that we just responded to what we were both exposed to.

I hear people talk about the idea of giving children whatever society feels "fits" each specific gender from the moment they are born. For example, many people believe that parents should not be painting their child's rooms blue or pink when they are born, and rather they should paint their room with a gender-neutral color. This, even in today's times, is progressive for parents because this has been something that has been considered "tradition" for years, and I have heard that being used as an argument. My response to that is simple: we no longer own slaves and gay marriage is being legalized, and both of these things "change" the "tradition" that has been upheld in this country for years.

People have also said that parents should not be giving their children toys that are specifically marketed towards specific genders, like racecars for boys and Barbie dolls for girls. Personally, I am able to relate to this overall idea that children should not be completely defined by their gender from the moment they enter the world. While I enjoyed playing with the cars my parents bought my brother and I, it was what I was exposed to at an early age.

My sister was born in 2001, and when she was little, my parents used to buy her Barbie dolls to play with. That was the first time Barbie dolls were brought into my house, and I was enamored with the dolls and houses they would live in. My sister and I would play with dolls together, to both the confusion and concern of my grandparents and, at one point, my parents. Even at a young age, I was intrigued by the idea that I could create another world with a plastic doll.

When I was in kindergarten, my mother bought me a Barbie doll with a SpongeBob SquarePants t-shirt on it after I asked her when I went shopping with her. Much to the dismay of my father and grandfather, who thought it might "make me gay," my mother bought the doll for me and let me bring it in to Show and Tell. I proudly showed my pants-peeing peers my new Barbie doll with an undertone that made it unclear if I thought of the doll as a child of my own or just my best friend that had horrible fashion sense because of her shirt. The other boys in the class brought in their whatever-ball and basketball shorts while I was rocking some jean shorts and a new top that my mom bought from Macy's and thought it was "kid chic."

When my brother entered kindergarten, he was one of the boys that brought their whatever-ball and worked some basketball shorts, and it would take a few years for my parents to see that they had two sons that were on the complete opposite ends of the spectrum. Although we were exposed to the same things as children, we just had opposite reactions towards them for whatever reason. We both liked cars, but I liked dolls and Kyle didn't, and Kyle liked sports and I didn't. At all.

◆

Reminiscing about sports is both hilarious and horrifying for me. I don't think like to think about the days when I was the kid that was forced to play sports but completely did not want to, but I really do like thinking about those days because they make hilarious stories.

My parents wanted Kyle and I to be exposed to different sports to see which ones we liked and wanted to continue playing. They didn't bargain for a kid that didn't want to play any sport at all, so they kept trying to put me on different teams in town to see if there was any sport I could have possibly enjoyed. They also didn't want us to not be active and keep our childhood chub, which didn't work (and you can tell by looking at some of my photos from the fifth grade). I don't remember playing flag football, but my parents signed me up to play when I was in the first grade. I only remember taking a group photo on a large rock, and I think I almost fell of the rock. Like the image of me falling off the rock, my football career went downhill, and I quit after one season.

My parents signed me up for baseball in the second grade, and my dad was one of the coaches. My poor father just wanted a boy to play catch with, and I was absolutely not that kid. I remember one of the practices where we were playing catch with a teammate, and the baseball lightly hit me in the face. Apparently, I didn't like that at all (which is kind of ironic considering my sexuality now, and that had to be said and I am not sorry for it), and I stormed off the field in tears. My embarrassed father had to run after me and bring me back to finish both that one practice and the entire season. I quit after the season finished, and I miss it as much as I miss middle school, so not at all.

The only sport I seemed to be able to keep up in was soccer, and that was only because I played for more than one year. My parents thought they hit the jackpot with soccer because I didn't leave, and they made me play at least one sport until I entered middle school, and soccer seemed to have been the least aggressive and offensive sport I knew (I didn't know about golf yet). I knew all I had to do was stand in the field and then sometimes look like I was running after the ball. But I found the practices to be brutal because it was hot outside and I was completely bored not playing the game. I even remember the coach asking the team who needed water within the first couple of minutes of the game. My hand shot up and the coach reluctantly pulled me aside for a rest. I was obviously the MVP of that game.

On the other end of the spectrum, Kyle was immediately drawn to sports, and he genuinely enjoyed playing all of them, which seemed to be more of a relief to my parents. In their defense, it is hard to see what kids like when they are so young. You can't look at a kid that barely knows how to read past a certain level and say, "This kid is going to be a writer!" No. Sports acted as both a test to see what your kid likes and a social gathering. Besides school, kids socialize at birthday parties and at sporting events. Little kids are not meeting at Starbucks to discuss the literary merit of *Twilight*. Maybe in the future… Maybe. But not today. And most definitely not yesterday.

Kyle was naturally good at sports, and he had the passion to play sports, passion that I was completely lacking. My parents always told me that I would be a good athlete if I was passionate about it, and I think they tell me that because I have a typical athlete's body: tall and wide. My body is completely wasted on me, and I'm sure someone who loves sports would give my body the abs it is lacking completely.

◆

Kyle has mostly guy friends, and I have majority girl friends. Kyle likes videogames, and I like videos and can do without the games. Kyle has a girlfriend, and I am single. Kyle is straight, and I am gay. Kyle plays sports, and I like the arts. We are just two different boys that happen to be from the same gene pool, and there are enough people that are confused when we tell people that we are related. I am even confused sometimes on how we are related.

Coming out to Kyle was a strange experience because Kyle, in many ways, represents the boys that I was completely afraid of but was also probably attracted to. I tend to be attracted to the straight athlete type, which will be one of my many downfalls in life. But, at the same time, I was completely afraid of the straight athletes. I have heard what they use to say about me, and let's just say that being gay made quite a few of them uncomfortable. What's funny is that many of these straight athletes get nervous, or at least used to get nervous, at the idea of a peer being gay because they assume that the gay kid automatically wanted to have sex with them. Don't flatter yourself, gents, but as a gay kid, I only wanted to have hookup with some of you, but in public I would say that I wanted to hookup with none of you as a political statement.

I came out to Kyle while we were both eating cheeseburgers and fries at the local fast food restaurant. Coming out to him was like facing some of the fears I had as a child. I remember being the kid in middle school, and even in high school, hoping to not be judged by the straight athletes and acting like I didn't care when I really did. For years, I thought of them as the enemy, and it took me a long time to realize that many of the straight athletes that scared me probably really didn't care about my, or anyone else's, sexuality as much as I thought they did. Besides that, we grew up, and we lose the mentality that developed in middle school (or at least I hoped). But, I don't know if I will ever completely get over the fear I had about what the straight athletes would say about me behind me back, or sometimes to my face. I remember one of them asking me on my Facebook profile if I was gay, and I quickly said no and deleted the message before anyone could see it. I was embarrassed, humiliated, and scared, and I wanted them to like me while also acting like I didn't care if they liked me or not.

Kyle was completely fine with my coming out, and he continues to be completely supportive and open. He asks me questions that I am no longer afraid to answer, and he has helped me link myself to the straight athlete world that I was, and sometimes still am, so completely afraid of. Kyle helped me realize that being a "straight athlete" does not define who you are as a person completely, as being a "gay thespian" does not completely define who I am as a person. I don't know if I will ever completely get over my fear of being judged by the straight athletes in the world, but I am taking the steps to get there slowly, and Kyle is helping me get there. For that, I will be forever grateful, even if he doesn't know it.

◆

One of the best things about having a brother that is on the complete opposite spectrum of boyhood is that we are able to see what we both do and connect in the way that many other do not because they do not see the opposite side of their own hobbies. In high school, Kyle was part of the football and baseball teams, and I was part of the theater program and was writing. In our school, and I'm sure in many schools, there was a large debate on the inequality of the recognition between sports and the arts. The theater program in our school has the most amount of students of any club in the school, and the program legitimately puts on two high quality shows every school year.

The sports program, specifically the football team, receives arguably receives the most attention in the school when you consider the amount of students that follow the sport compared to any other club, including other sports, in the school. The team has won the State Championship, which was well deserved and well earned, two years in a row, and the football games prove to be one of the largest social gatherings for most of the student body. Relating back to theater, the company has received multiple nominations and wins for multiple theater-related awards from the state, which are also well deserved and well earned. Something both the football team and theater company have in common is that they have to entertain a crowd when they have a performance or game. Yes, the football team is playing a sport it is passionate about. And yes, the theater is putting on a show they are passionate about, whether an audience is there or not. But, there is an audience and crowd that pays to see entertainment, whether it is to see two people tackle each other for a ball or a teenager trying to both remember lines from Shakespeare plays and act well while doing it. No matter what each group is doing, they have an audience to please. Another thing they both have in common is that they both work extremely hard at their craft and/or sport, and that deserves to be recognized, as each sports teams and clubs do.

Without a doubt, there is an unbalance in the attention the arts and sports receive. Everyone knows this, and everyone who tries to deny this would either be a little delusional or a little naïve. Sports, especially football, are known to be a pastime in American history, and the passion the fans have for the sport hasn't changed. Watching a show is a completely difference experience. Football is a sport where fans scream and yell and chant for their favorite team. There is something to root for, and there is something to heckle. It brings people with a common interest together. There are no teams to root for in theater. There is one stage where you watch the "action" happen. There is silence in the audience because a performance is watching in front of you. But there is passion in a different way than the passion you see in a sports game. People with a common interest are brought together to watch something amazing unfold. And the problem doesn't lie with either the theater group or the football team. Rather, it lies with the audience and their own interests.

We can't force people to enjoy something they don't. My parents couldn't force me to like sports, and they couldn't force me to stop playing with dolls. My parents can't force my brother to go on stage and perform a play, but they also couldn't stop him from wanting to play sports.

The great thing Kyle and I have together is that we appreciate each other's craft because we have lived seeing each other perform each other's crafts over the years. For that, we are both lucky, and seeing us perform our own crafts makes us wonder how we are born into the same family. But, as I think about it, that is the problem with us as a body of students. There is a discord between many members of sports teams and many members of the arts because many of us think that we can never really be related to each other as students in one school. We can never be similar to each other because like completely different things. Because of this, many people on each side cannot see how similar we really are. We are all just people that are passionate about something, whether it is a sports team, an arts program, a school club, grades, partners, friends, family, etc.

I recognize that Kyle works out for hours every day to perfect his craft, as he recognizes that I spend hours working on my own craft. We have a mutual respect for each other that is lacking with many other students. Instead of focusing on how different we all are because of the hobbies we do, we have to start focusing on how we really are more similar than we think we are, and we might start recognizing more of a change. And then we can tell ourselves that we all might be from the same, or at least a similar, breed after all.

◆

My father always wanted a boy to play catch with. Ultimately, that kid isn't me, and I feel bad that I was not the kid he expected me to be. He found that kid in Kyle, not to say that being the kid that your parents thought you might be is a bad thing at all. My father, while reluctant to accept me for who I really am at first, ultimately got to that place of acceptance and understanding. I hope he is proud to have two sons that are completely different but love each other all the same.

My father and I got into a fight with my mother recently, and my coming out to both of them was brought up in the fight. In defense of my mother, my father admitted that he originally thought to himself, "What did I do wrong?" when I came out to him. It took him longer to accept me than my mother did. I can only imagine what went through my father's head the moment I came out to him. Why did I let my son play with dolls? Why I did let him quit sports? Why didn't I play catch with him more? Why does he not like the same things I like? Why isn't he more like his brother? What could I have done differently to prevent this?

He was scared. I was scared, and despite being scared for different reasons, our reactions were ultimately the same. It doesn't matter how Kyle and I were raised. We were exposed to the same things, and we just reacted differently, which is how the arts and sports become what they are in the first place. We are all just reacting to what we have experienced in our lives, and we are being lead by our passions. But, there was an acceptance that Kyle and I had for each other. There was an acceptance my father and I had for each other. He couldn't change me, whether it was

I not liking sports or I not liking women. But he accepted me for who I was, and he knew I would work hard at whatever I did in my life. And like my father did, accepting each other for who we are is what moves us forward as a community. We just have to open our minds up to do this.

Five Things I Learned My Freshman Year of High School

Freshman year is never an easy time, except for maybe the hot kids. But, here are the five things I learned my freshman year of high school that I wish I knew before I entered the smelly fish tank that is high school.

1. It isn't a myth that the upperclassmen don't like you very much.

I wish I were lying. I wish I could tell you that high school movies were wrong, and each grade just liked each other. I heard about "Freshman Friday," which was apparently the day where freshmen were stuffed into lockers liked they would be in an old Disney Channel Original Movie. Luckily, it is not this bad, or at least it wasn't this bad in the high school I attended. Actually, I felt that maybe I could walk among the school as a freshman like I've been there for years. Unfortunately, I received a rude awakening when the first pep rally of the year occurred before Thanksgiving break. It was all fun and games until the junior class on the other side of the gymnasium verbally harassed us by chanting "FRESHMEN SUCK" over and over again until a teacher made them stop.

2. Your style might change, and this might be a great thing.

If you were anything like me, you were working sweatpants and oversized jeans every day to school in the name of fashion. And if you were anything like me, you grew up and decided that your look was no longer working for you. Or maybe, that look still works for you, and that is totally fine.

3. Not everyone is a super model in high school, and the hallway is not New York Fashion Week.

Don't let TV shows about high school (like *90210*, I'm calling you out) let you believe that everyone looks drop dead gorgeous every day. No. No. Not everyone, especially teenagers, has the cash to buy outfits you would find on the runway and wear them to math class. Also, not everyone has a makeup artist that will make you look picture-perfect every day. And your hair is not always going to look like Jesus washed and styled it for you. No, sometimes your hair is going to look like you are styled it with a stick of butter and glue because you had a bad day. Sometimes, sweats and sneakers is the day's outfit because it is comfortable and that's more of a priority than looking like a model every day. The hallway is not going to look like New York Fashion Week, and sometimes it is going to look like New York Fashion Week has a crack problem, especially during midterms and finals week.

4. Friend groups can change in high school. THIS IS NORMAL.

And if you are like me, then you might be one of the reasons your friend group can change. I was psychotic freshman year (more on this later), and I had trouble with one friend that was in our group. In many cases, a friend group changing, whether someone leaves or someone joins or you leave or you join, is normal and many times a side effect of transitioning from one school to another.

5. High school is so much better than middle school.

Yes, freshman year is the year of heckling, and you are transitioning from one phase of your life to another. But, there is nothing better than realizing middle school is over. You may see this during your middle school graduation, or you may see this at the end of your freshman year. It will hit you when you least expect it. You will be walking down the hallway and you smile at someone out of pure kindness and they respond with a nasty look, and you will think, "Middle school was so much worse."

Fakeianity:

The Time I Was a Christian and Then Not

My parents are what I call "fake Catholics," but I know other people would consider them "cafeteria Catholics." They only want to go to Church on Christmas and Easter, and they don't believe in every doctrine the Church preaches. So, I guess they are really more the "simpleton Catholics" because they have a basic belief in God and continue to have souls and compassion for human beings that may like the same gender or get divorces or get an abortion. In my mind, the ones who don't have compassion or understanding of anything outside of the Jesus bubble are what I refer to as "crazy Catholics." That's right, religious sects of Christianity are not just divided by Protestant, Catholic, and others I don't care to think about. No. They are divided by how Catholic I feel that they are, like any of them really care about how I view their relationship with their religion.

My parents put my siblings and myself in Catholic education since we each started kindergarten. Thankfully, my parents didn't put us in Catholic school, even though I wouldn't have known nor cared if they did this since I would have been so little. The Catholic school near my house, which also served as the Catholic education program for everyone who didn't attend Catholic school, had this dark aura to me that I noticed since I was a child. I think this was because the walls were painted a dark yellow that looked like the kind of urine that would send you to the hospital or even just the look of a normal hearty vomit, and the school always has a strange smell. Of course, this has nothing to do with the actual religious affiliation with the school, as it was just some bad décor that I would stare at instead of doing the opening prayer with the rest of the class.

My parents originally sent us to the Catholic education meetings every month, and then my parents got super lazy and signed us up for the summer program that only lasted a week and would have follow up meetings every few months. My parents thought it would work better scheduling-wise if we just "got it over with" (their words not mine- ok mine as well) over the summer, as if the schedules of elementary school kids in the early 2000s wee too unmanageable to handle one meeting every month. But, I never complained about the lack of Catholic education that was happening every year. For me, it was like ripping a bandage off. I would "get it over with" and finish the week, and then wait until next year where I would have another boring week not memorizing any Bible stories and not even pretending like I knew them.

Ok, fine. I am making it sound like I was a bad Catholic, which isn't even true. I prayed as a child, and I would try and "talk" to God whenever I had a frivolous issue. When you are in religious education, you briefly talk about other religions, but you are always taught that your religion is ultimately the one that is "correct." So, why wouldn't I believe in God and pray to him? This is also why I have some understanding for people that bring religion into politics, even though even writing about frustrates and even angers me. We are taught that our religion is correct and the universal truth, so how could we not take that into our politics? It's too hard for many people to separate because many people just believe that there is no reason to separate it.

So, I would pray whenever I did something "bad," and we had to go through steps in Church over the years that I once learned were just the Sacraments you needed to go through to be confirmed to the Church. I was baptized as a baby, which sounds a pretty unpleasant for a baby to go through but we get to wear cute outfits. I confessed my sins to the Priest, where I told him the stories of the few times I cursed and one story where I told him a urinal in the bathroom was running and I didn't tell a teacher that it was overflowing (the Priest seemed both impressed and confused by me being that honest and telling that random tale). I had my first Holy Communion, where I tasted "Jesus" for the first time in the form of a stale wafer (Catholics-back me up on this one. I know it's your God but don't act like this isn't true) and his "blood" in the form of wine that I thought was sour grape juice.

I make fun of it all now, but I didn't have much knowledge of other religions back then. Like I said before, your respective religious educators teach you that your religion is the correct one, and why wouldn't they? A Priest is not going to tell you that the religion "may" be wrong. No. By the way, the Priest didn't even teach the classes. Instead, keeping it embarrassingly suburbanized, the housewives/power moms would teach the class. The perk about having these mothers teach the classes was that sometimes they would bring food with them to the class. I remember only being excited to attend class one year because one mother brought bread with her for the class, and that says a lot about both my religious pursuits and my eating habits.

But, I digress. Anyway, I had one view of religion when I was that age. Actually, I did have some knowledge of Judaism, as it was the most common religion practiced among the children besides Christianity, but, again, we were told that Judaism was totally wrong with the implication that a Bat and Bar Mitzvah was just a Sweet 16 with a different name and some Hebrew sprinkled in the Challah bread that was served (with the word, "Shalom," which is probably the only Hebrew word I understand). But, in middle school, I became close friends with my best friend/sister but not really/pain in the ass, Tyler. Her family was agnostic, and she was raised being able to practice or not practice any religion that interested her. In high school, she would tell me about her atheist beliefs, which both fascinated me and frightened me. *What do you mean there*

is no heaven? Where do we go once we die? What about a
hell? Will I go there if I don't believe in it anymore? Oh,
well, I guess that contradicts itself a bit.

Tyler likes to bring up how I would try and
convince her that heaven was most definitely real and we
would be able to go there once we died. She would ask,
"Well, how does everyone fit in heaven?" I responded with,
"Um... I don't know... Our bodies don't go but our souls
go there and we will all fit in there and be super happy." It
was like I was giving a presentation that was going south
because the computer shut off in the middle of me
speaking. I might have had some sort of argument, but it
was ruined with statements like, "You can do whatever you
want in heaven! You can go on God's computer or watch
television and DVR your favorite shows and eat all the
food you want because you won't gain weight!" Yes, I had
day dreams about what heaven would be like as a child
because Catholics kept telling me that the afterlife is even
better than life itself (which sounds absolutely terrible for a
child, the closest thing that is fresh out of the oven of life
besides a baby, to hear), so I just thought of cool things that
heaven would have. But, I love how the idea of heaven has
changed for people over the years. Can we just think about
how at one point heaven was just a place where people of
the Civil War could just hang out and relax after fighting a
brutal war? Now, in the early 2000s, heaven is just a
wonderland for spoiled suburban kids. And what did my
ass do to deserve that? Oh yeah, not listen to the sermons in
Church. That's what.

So, Tyler didn't buy the timeshare I was selling, and she shot my proposal down like a bird she was hunting that she finally caught, and she continues to be proud of the bird she hunted. I am now an atheist, and she gives herself credit for bringing me to the other side.

Before I was an atheist, I was atheism's innocent and shy cousin, an agnostic. I told my parents that I was no longer Catholic the same way I came out to them, in the kitchen when they least expected it. Apparently, being a dramatic child, I just had to tell my parents big news in the kitchen when they just thought they would have a nice dinner in solitude.

Here are some examples of the news I have told my parents in the kitchen:

1. I am gay, and it is not a phase.
2. I am not Catholic. I am Agnostic.
3. I am not an Agnostic anymore. I am an Atheist.
4. Michael Jackson scares me, no matter how much of a good singer he is.
5. Casey Anthony killed her child, and I will not even listen to the argument that she didn't.
6. Speaking of children, I am adopting kids instead of having my own.
7. I am attracted to black men.

With the news that I became an Agnostic, I told my parents that I didn't want to be confirmed to the Church. My parents refused to budge on this, and they told me that I could make my own religious decisions when I turned eighteen. So basically, I could be agnostic but I still had to attend Church. Oh, and I was supposed to be confirmed in about a year. And my parents not only wanted me to stay and finish my religious education because I have been doing it for so many years, but it was also because they spent money on the classes and they didn't want their money to go to waste with my quitting. In my own defense, my Church kept students for an extra two years before allowing them to be confirmed to the Church, and the Confirmation meetings consisted of playing with rocks and silently judging other students that I knew were as religious as my middle finger.

I agreed to stay in the Confirmation meetings, as if I had choice in the matter, and I did my usual routine until the day I knew I could put up some sort of fight. That day was the meeting that focused on abstinence. Ok, let's be honest here. The Catholic Church does not, theoretically, support same-sex marriage. As a gay teenager that happens to also be a little dramatic, I did not feel welcomed in the Church, which is something I argued to my parents when I originally proposed to them that I quit my Catholic education. They understood this argument, but they still didn't want their money to go to waste. Also, my parents believe in giving their kids some sort of religious education for some sort of structure and then make your own decisions when you become an adult. But, I thought that this meeting might change their minds. I mean, this is Catholics talking about anything related to sex? I'm sure they would say something that must be, at the very least, somewhat offensive to the LGBT community. I both craved and dreaded the idea of going to the meeting that night, which sounds awful of me, but I was also just curious to see what they had to say about people like me.

I walk into the meeting with a fire in my ass that was most definitely unholy for multiple reasons. I was ready to hear what the Catholics had to say about to say about sex and what not to do about it. I sit down in the Church pew without bowing down to pray, which was my own form of rebellion against the "man." A man, presumably in his thirties, walked into the Church and began telling the overly horny and hormonal sophomore class about the potential beauty of not having sex until you get married. Not sitting well with the kids, we had the opportunity to ask different questions anonymously by writing the question on a notecard and placing it in a bin. Mr. No Sex Until Marriage read the questions out loud, and one was about his views on LGBT marriage and gay sex. Mr. NSUM told us that he felt that "you can't help you are attracted to, but you can control how you react to that attraction." As an anti-Catholic looking to make a case, I got what I wanted. As someone who is part of the LGBT youth and has yet to enter the "real world," I was completely offended.

Who was this man to tell me that I could "control the way I act?" This was a man who had three little children, and the idea of him teaching his kids this made me sick. While this was not the worst comment I have ever heard about the LGBT community (nothing will beat someone saying "it's disgusting" in the middle of class), but I was truly annoyed that he would say something like that to impressionable youth. To imply that someone should marry someone of the opposite gender while really being attracted to someone of the same gender *Brokeback Mountain* style just sounds like a completely miserable life.

I went home with a new fire in my ass in an even more unholy way, and I told my parents how offended I was by what that man said to everyone in the church. My parents, eating some salmon they bought from the supermarket, told me that they understood my concerns, but I should still finish just to get it over with. Similar to the way I felt when Mr. NSUM said what he said, it felt like my parents cut me up like a piece of sushi with their words. My plan wasn't working, which was already upsetting, and I was genuinely hurt by what the way they handled the situation.

I ultimately confirmed to the church in May of my sophomore year, and I acted like it was a chore rather than a day of celebration. I frowned in a very cheesy teenage angst-y way for most of the celebration, and I was one of the first people to hit the snack table after the whole thing was over. 1. I was hungry because food babies don't look hot in a suit. 2. It was another form of rebellion, as I didn't want the church to hold me back from eating a very stale chocolate chip cookie.

Following my parent's promise, I continued to attend church every Christmas and Easter until I turned eighteen years old. My last attendance of church, at least for now, was Christmas of 2014. I sat down in the pew, knowing that it would be my last attendance. I thought about my own beliefs while listening to the priest. *Do I really want to leave this? Am I just being stubborn?*

I don't know what I will believe ten or twenty years from now. For all I know, I could one day turn back to my Christianity and go back to Church, but I knew, at least for now, this just wasn't for me. It wasn't coming from a place of hurt or anger or rebellion. It was coming from my own religious (or I guess non-religious) awakening: I am not a Catholic, and that is ok.

◆

I was sixteen years old when I found out that both my grandmother from my father's side and my grandfather from my mother's side were diagnosed with cancer. My grandmother had skin cancer while my grandfather had lung cancer. I have never experienced death in my family before. The only death that was close to my family was a family friend that passed away years ago, and I was too young to really understand that she was gone forever. Other than that, I am lucky to be able to have all of my grandparents alive throughout my childhood.

These two cancer diagnoses were a blow to my family, especially because my grandfather originally did not want to get treatment. My grandfather, a tall and tough English and Irish war veteran, smoked for most of his life, and it led him to get cancer in his lungs. The doctors wanted him to go into surgery to remove the cancer, but my grandfather was reluctant to go through with the surgery. He wanted to let the cancer run its course rather than treat it, which is something my family members couldn't really wrap their heads around. My grandfather felt he lived a full life, as he was in his early seventies at that point and living a retired life with my grandmother and his post-midlife crisis motorcycle in Florida.

My grandmother, a short and petite Colombian interior designer who lives only about a half an hour from my family and I, started getting treatment for her skin cancer that consisted of intense chemotherapy and radiation around the same time my grandfather was deciding whether to get his own treatment or not. Eventually, both my grandmother and my grandfather went through with their treatments, and my grandmother went into remission after many chemotherapy sessions and my grandfather's cancer was removed completely in surgery.

◆

I think of my grandmother picking up my brother, sister, and I to take us to her apartment to sleep over. We would go to the bookstore, where my grandmother would let me buy the DVD of the shows I was obsessing over as a child (which consisted of marathons of *Beverly Hills, 90210*, a show that one should never watch to try and get an accurate representation of high school). I slept on my grandmother's air mattress in her living room and watched my DVDs while drinking the soda she bought from the store just for us because she always looked forward to having us over. The next morning, she would go buy breakfast for us, and we would stay until the mid-afternoon when she would take us to the store to go post-sleepover shopping and swap with my parents, who would wait in the parking lot.

This went on for years, until my brother, sister, and I told my parents, that we were too old to have sleepovers at her house. We wanted to hang out with our friends on the weekends. We had homework to get done on Sunday. We wanted to sleep in our own beds. We have plans Saturday night so we couldn't cancel them to "hang out" with our grandmother. My grandmother was happy and content with seeing her grandchildren happy and content, from the moment we played in the feces-stained McDonald's playpen to the car ride back to the store to do the swapping of adult figures.

Even when she got sick, my grandmother always smiled when she saw us. She would come to the house in her wig of the week and an outfit that made her look like the Queen of a forbidden land that contained subjects with an eclectic fashion sense and an aesthetic of old curtains and Colombian tablecloths. My grandmother is the epitome of the hash tag #WorkBitch, as she always works her look of the day, whether it is a sassy wig that looks like a costume wig for the costume, "Sexy House Maid," or her shaved head with the little hairs growing back that represents how far she has gone and how far she is going to continue going. The cancer is not winning the game of life, as my grandmother is fighting hard to not let that happen. Her eyebrows are already covered, as in what I assume to be typical Colombian fashion, those are shaved and she has some tattooed red lines instead. Your move, cancer.

72

◆

I think of my grandfather sitting on my couch on Christmas Eve and drinking scotch in a coffee mug. My two grandmothers come to my house every Christmas from Florida. Their daily routine consists of waking up, eating, napping, watching CNN, napping, eat lunch, napping, watching more CNN, drinking, eating, and sleeping for the night. For my grandfather, sprinkle in smoking every hour or two. Evidently, cancer was not in the cards for my grandfather, and he was not going to let it take over his life, or so I would like to believe. I think of his stories, where he would tell us about the experiences he had when he was sixteen and seventeen years old. He was a talented musician, a war veteran, and somehow threw in a wife and two children. His stories fill me with joy and embarrassment, as I spent my sixteenth year trying to come up with a clever hash tag for Twitter and trying to get boys to fall in love with me while knowing they never would.

When my grandfather originally decided not to get treatment, I was both shocked and not surprised at all. I thought, *Why wouldn't you want to get treatment? Why would you choose to suffer and potentially end your life earlier than you can?* But, my grandfather just felt that he already lived a pretty full life. Truthfully, my grandfather did everything he wanted to do, or so I think. He lived his life to the fullest, from passionately working as a pilot to raising two girls. Now, he spends his time napping and watching television. I can only imagine what his feelings are when it comes to his life at this point. For people at my age and older, the life of a senior citizen sounds both promising and scary. You have the freedom to relax after a seemingly full life, and that is the best-case scenario. But, as I'm sure my grandfather thought, what more is there to life? You go from working and being busy to having the freedom of napping and going to the supermarket to kill time. What more is there to experience? Where do you go from there? My grandfather traveled, as he lived in England and traveled around the world because of his career. What more is there to do?

Then, he gets cancer. Does he try to stop it from running its course, or does he take it as a sign that his time is over? But, my family looked at it in a way that most would: What about the ones you are leaving behind? When you are gone, what does the mean for the ones that are still here?

◆

I don't believe in a heaven or a hell or an afterlife. I believe that once we die, we just no longer exist. I don't believe I will see anyone I knew in my life ever again once they die, and it makes me sad to think about this at times. Being raised Catholic, I was promised that I would see everyone I knew in my life in a place that was better than the world we live in now. I was promised that the last time I saw my loved ones on Earth was not really the last time I would see them again. I was taught that the ones I loved would be able to watch me on Earth. It took me years to stop believing in this, but I eventually did.

I talked to a family member about my beliefs, and it became a debate on what is true and what is not regarding the afterlife. We won't know until we die, but we still try and argue one side and another.

My family member pleaded to me, "This can't be it. This can't be all there is. There has to be more after this. It can't just end."

This line has stuck with me, and it has broken my heart at times. Part of me wishes I still believed in something after death, but another part of me is content with my beliefs because it makes me appreciate the life I am living more than I did before. I notice many religious people focus more on the possible afterlife than the life they are living now. I cannot look at the afterlife with the thought of, "What if?" because I already do that in my life here. What if I become famous? What if I never find someone that loves me? What if I am not truly happy in the life that I am living now?

We can be the happiest people on Earth, but we always want more. It's just human nature to want more than we already have. In a perfect world, nobody is diagnosed with cancer. We could just die in our sleep in the most peaceful way without any suffering. For some, a perfect world is one where death doesn't exist. It doesn't happen, and we all just age gracefully together. I see that enough on television shows and movies, where we fantasize about dying and returning in some form or another, whether it is through the resurrection of our bodies or just becoming a house plant.

My grandmother had to get more treatment in October and November of 2014, and she stayed at the hospital for over a month because the radiation treatments were too intense to allow her to go back home. My grandfather, cancer free, is smoking again. Smoking is both an addiction and part of my grandfather's daily routine. He has been doing it for most of life, and cancer is not going to stop him from doing it. He is playing with his life, but that is his choice. It is the same choice we make when we get in the car every day and drive. Smoking is just not as common as driving is. And we just view smoking and driving differently in terms of endangering our lives.

I don't think I will see my grandparents when they die, whether it is from cancer or anything else. I don't think I will see my brother and sister again when they die, and I have shared a home with them for eighteen years. I don't think I will see my parents again when they die, and they have provided that home I have lived in. I don't think I will see my friends again when they die, and they have helped me become the person I am today.

By no longer practicing a religion, I have gained a different perspective on life. Instead of worrying and dreaming about a life that is seemingly "better" than this one, I have decided to focus on the life I am living now and work on being content with my one life here. I am learning to cherish the moments I have had with my family and friends, even the ones that seem unimportant. What was just a sleepover with my grandmother has turned into a cherish childhood memory, when things were a little simpler for everyone. With my mindset and my new view, time has become more valuable than I ever thought before.

I don't know where I will stand when my family members die, as I am lucky enough to still have my immediate family and my grandparents and close relatives still in my life. I want to say that my beliefs will stay the same, but I cannot promise that. I once was a Catholic that was questioning but accepting the beliefs I was taught to an Atheist that has a completely different view on the meaning life. I don't look at it only as a belief that has been changed by my friends and my environment, but I also look at it as growth and being able to come up with my own beliefs instead of only accepting the beliefs someone told me were the correct ones.

Tal-Order:

The Many Times I Was Kicked Out of a Friend's Dressing Room and Cried About It

I stand at six feet and one inch tall, which makes it extremely difficult to hide. Believe me, I have tried. My height goal is really more five feet and eleven inches, but I also want a lifetime supply of fried chicken and we can't always get what we want.

I remember always wishing to somehow change my body to make myself fit in more with my group of friends. I wished I were shorter than I was. I wished I were more petite than I was. I wished I was not the boy that was different than my friends, but rather I wanted to be the same as my other girlfriends and be able to hide myself from the idea of human differences.

I tried to be different than my friends, but nothing worked. A doctor I visited told me before freshman year of high school that I would have to wear a back brace if I keep hunching over because apparently I was hunching dangerously low. Of course, being a teenager, my main concern was not my health. No. It's all fun and games until they threaten you with a back brace. My immediate reaction was, *Oh my God what will everyone think when I come to school with a giant back brace?!* Not only am I a teenager, I am also a dramatic person, so I acted like I was becoming Edward Scissorhands with a back brace that was made by a lovely and lonely scientist.

Nevertheless, there were times where I didn't feel different than my friends, or at least the feelings were not as severe as they sometimes were. I remember a specific situation freshman year, where I went to the mall with my friends for our occasional mall trip. Look, options are limited when you are fourteen years old. You can't drive, so you have to rely on your parents to take you places, and that is usually reserved for the weekend unless you have really kind parents that have apparently nothing else to do than take their child and friends to their mall in the middle of the afternoon on a Wednesday. So, we had our mall trip on a Saturday afternoon that lasted until early Saturday night, as my mother was worried about the supposed gang activity that occurs in suburban malls. Thank you, Google.

While other kids were shopping at middle school hubs like Hot Topic to try on t-shirts their parents would absolutely hate, my friends and I decided to go to Macy's to look at the most hideous clothes they were selling for middle aged moms that grandmothers would describe "hip" and "eccentric." Very grandma chic, and we picked some of the outfits to try on.

I joined my friends in the dressing rooms with their senior-citizen-goes-on-a-cruise outfits, and we laughed as I watched them try on the clothes. Moments after the second outfit was put on, a tall and skinny woman, whose name I remember was Tal, waited outside the dressing room until we came out, and she spoke the few words that I have never forgotten.

"I'm sorry, but boys are not allowed to go in the dressing rooms with girls."

Boom. Tal dropped the bomb that destroyed my fifteen-year-old heart. Even though I knew it was store policy and not a rule she came up with on her own, I was offended. *What does she think my friends and I are going to do in the dressing rooms? What does she think I am going to do to the girls in the dressing rooms?* I felt isolated, and I felt singled out of my own friend group. I was embarrassed, as something so innocent turned into a possible situation of inappropriate behavior because of a store policy. I wanted to hide in one of the gowns that the store was selling and cry. I wanted to scream at poor Tal, "I'm gay and I have no interest in these girls whatsoever, so why am I being kicked out like I am some sexual predator!" Again, the dramatic fifteen-year-old brain comes into play, and it spits up statements like that. Tal couldn't control what the store policies were, as I couldn't control that I am a boy and therefore being different than my friends', who were girls.

I walked out of the dressing room with sympathetic looks on my friends' faces, but we continued playing around with the clothes. But, it wasn't the same as before. Instead of being together in one room and innocently playing around, there was a barrier between us through the form of a rusty dressing room door. And that door was a reminder that, no matter how hard we tried to ignore them, there were clear differences between my friends and myself that could not be hidden.

◆

My friends liked to have sleepovers when we were in eighth grade and then freshmen in high school, much to my dismay. I always dreaded the weekend sleepovers that my girlfriends had because I could never stay and sleep over with them. My parents believed, at the time, that sleepovers should only be between people of the same gender. They were new to understanding the world of gay teenagers, but they stuck to their beliefs that girls should only have sleepovers with girls and boys should only have sleepovers with boys, which is completely ironic when you think about it.

I remember sitting and crying to my best friend, Tyler, about not being able to attend these coveted sleepovers. Looking back on it, I realize how silly these sleepovers really were, as sleepovers really are just friends hanging out in the night and doing anything but sleeping. But, I never looked at it in a simplistic way. To me, sleepovers are a time for bonding and connecting with your friends, and I wasn't able to participate. Sleepovers are for sharing your thoughts about everything from your lack of sex life at fourteen years old to how much you dislike a certain teacher. Sleepovers are meant to bring close people even closer, and I just felt left out from my friends. Sleepovers were one of the barriers between my friends and I, as I could never attend them. It was the wall that was the reminder to my friends and I that I was different, even more different than my friends were to each other.

My freshman year of high school became a year of self-loathing and cry sessions, and at times (most times) it just became pathetic and embarrassing. I tried so hard to be the same as my friends, and when I couldn't do it, I chose to cry and hate myself for trying to do the impossible. I couldn't help that I was a boy, just as my friends couldn't help that they were girls. We connected with each other because of our personalities and not because of our genders.

I hated myself, and I took it out on my friends. Specifically, there was one friend that I turned on, and I look back with some shame because of the way I acted. My friend and I were having arguments over frivolous things, but I felt that she wasn't totally accepting of my sexuality even though there was little evidence to prove such a statement. But, she was also considered the "leader" of our group, as she had the most outspoken personality, and she connected us all together originally.

I wrote a childish blog about my "freedom" from her (re. I was/am a dramatic person), as many teenagers tend to act like every situation they are in is some sort of "liberation" from society's expectations and demands. Now, when I think about our relationship, I think we had many issues because I felt that she reminded me constantly of the differences between us that shamed and hurt me, and I wasn't able to handle it. I was looking for a way to push aside my own feelings because it is apparently easier to deal with feelings when you are actually not dealing with them at all.

The peak moment of the emotional roller coaster that was my freshman year was actually during the summer before sophomore year began. My friend invited my two other friends, including Tyler, to a weekend in her family's beach house. We were all watching a show together, and I overheard her asking Tyler in private whether she wanted to go or not. For any normal human being, this would be taken as someone trying to be considerate to another person by not saying it in front of them. For me, as someone who's brain was downing in tears and oddly emotional sweat, I took this as I was being singled out once again and my friends were trying to leave me out of a beach trip. Ugh! (re. EMOTIONAL).

This led to a night of Tyler literally hearing my sobbing and dry heaving on my bed while drowning my cell phone. I looked like an Emmy award-winning actor just doing a day's work on my soap opera because my mother died, or I looked like Kim Kardashian when she was crying because she lost her earring in the ocean on her vacation. Not cute, as I assume one of the Kardashians would say to me. By the way, my crying session was so Reality-TV worthy it was ridiculous. All I needed was a camera crew and a believer, and my show would have kicked the Kardashians back to Oprah (God)-knows-where.

I sobbed on my bed for about two hours (that is the time Tyler gave me), and then I peacefully fell asleep (passed out) on my bed. Only later did I realize that Tyler, at one point, took a bathroom break and got a drink of water while leaving the phone in her bedroom. So, I was sobbing to no one at one point, which is only not shameful when something severe actually happens in your life.

By the time sophomore year started, I was on the blissful road of getting my shit together. But, the road itself would be shit unless I actually started with the basics: appreciating myself and my worth little by little. Instead of hating everything I couldn't change, I had to start appreciating those differences and accepting that I couldn't change the unchangeable. It was a slow process that I am still currently working on. I still care what people think about me, no matter how much I don't want to. I want people to think I'm funny, kind, and smart. I want people to like this essay I am writing. It is so much easier to ignore your own feelings about yourself when you can focus on other people liking you and telling you how great you are. We all want to hear it because it's just human nature.

I accepted the fact that I am going to be different than my friends for my own reasons, as we are all truly different from each other in our own ways. I couldn't go to the sleepovers that my friends had when I was fourteen years old. How long am I supposed to hold on to that fact? My friends and I stay at each other's houses now, so things have changed in that regard. Yeah, I don't wear the same clothes as my friends, and most of my friends and I don't share the same downstairs region of our bodies. But, there is nothing I can do about that. Over time, I accepted the differences between my friends and I, and I have become proud to be different than my friends and stand out more, even during the times where I am reminded of this in the most unexpected of ways.

The journey of accepting yourself is a lifelong journey, and I didn't think it would be this way. I thought sophomore year was the year I truly accepted myself and actually *loved* myself, but I didn't know that I still had (and still have) so much to learn. As the years pass, I grow and appreciate myself more and more. I went from someone who thought that something was wrong them, was weird, lonely, strange, different to someone that is funny, kind, smart, while still being different and finally embracing it. I hopped in the car of self-acceptance, but I am still miles away from my destination, and I am ready for the drive.

Welcome to Camp, and Leave Your Wand In the Car

I got my first job the summer before my sophomore year in high school. My parents made me get one not only because I would be making money, but they also didn't like the idea of me sitting on my ass all summer long. My parents are both very hard working, as they are lawyers. They have worked hard their own lives, and my siblings and I are lucky enough to be supported by them because of the amount of work they do every day. Since a fair amount of teenagers, especially in an upper middle class suburb, think the world revolves around them, I didn't always see this. But, I didn't mind getting a job, as I liked the idea of being to earn a check for myself and feel a little more independent, or at least as independent as one can be at fifteen years old.

I began working as a counselor at my town's local day camp from the end of June and finished by the end of July. The kids allowed to attend the camp ranged from kids entering first grade to kids entering seventh grade, and you were able to start working there by ninth grade. So I laughed at the fact that some of the "campers" were only a few years younger than I was, and I already had trouble establishing some control over a group of people.

The first year I started working at the camp, I was watching a group of rambunctious and very energetic first grade boys. I mean, wow. The amount of energy those boys had was insane, and it is giving me anxiety just writing about it now. I remember thinking that some of the parents totally put some cocaine in their cereal so they would be energetic at camp and then just pass out by the time they came home. Too far? Sorry, Sheila (a name I made up that is a mother of a kid I probably never had).

The group of kids was coming in one by one on the first day of camp. I am sitting down with my extremely bright yellow t-shirt/uniform on (assuming the camp wanted a bright feel that would make the parents feel like they were sending their kids to). Together, the counselors looked like a bunch of fresh lemons, so I guess seeing the color made the kids even more energetic. Could you imagine the camp counselors wearing black t-shirts to camp? Oh my god, the anxiety. I already had a sweating issue for basically a year in high school (I still sweat pretty easily but I don't like to talk about it, so don't bring it up), and the idea of wearing black t-shirts on a hot summer day would turn my body into a slip n' slide, and that is not a good look for parents who are dropping their kids off to a seemingly safe summer camp.

I sit down on the first day with a classmate of mine, and I immediately sense some trouble. Honestly, both my classmate and I are shy writers. Actually, I am not that shy. So that's not totally true. But I have total trouble taking control any group of people. I am not even able to make dinner plans without asking everyone where they want to possibly eat instead of making the decision. Am I really capable of handling a group of first graders? Sophomore year me thought I certainly could, but I really knew I couldn't, so I am the perfect candidate for this job. *As long as no kids get hurt or die, I'm good*, I thought. All I had to do was get through a few hours of glorified babysitting and the kids would get home safely and parents would give a nice tip. No issues, no problem. Then, camp actually started.

The kids roll in, and many of them seem to be little athletes of the future. Many of them looked like middle school boys, as they walked in with basketball shorts wore their cologne: I am a first grader and I haven't showered in five days because my mom can't make me do anything. Nice. Comforting. Luckily, I smelled fine, and I apparently thought that everyone would understand that people in charge always smell the best in the room. Not having much to work with, my simple deodorant would do just fine.

I am seeing the same kind of kids, which is perfectly fine with me because they all seemed to be friends with each other. *Perfect*. Little kids that are friends with each other tend to wreak havoc on the entire group *Cheaper By The Dozen* style (or channeling the 90s film *Problem Child*) or stick with each other and don't cause trouble except for the occasional "I fell and I need a bandage" routine. But, these kids were multiplying by the minute. We were warned about having a large group of kids, but we ended up having give or take twenty kids in one group. Luckily, my classmate and I had another counselor with us who looked like someone that would take charge.

I thought the kids are done coming in when I see one more coming out of the corner of my eye. This kid was different than the rest already. I could already tell. He walked in with some "trendy" blue shorts on, a t-shirt, and he didn't smell like he just came from football practice. He had a mushroom haircut, which was similar to the one my younger brother worked in the early 2000s, and he had the cheeks the size of tiny melons. His name was Jake, and he was refreshing, and I was excited but also nervous to see how he would interact with the group. There were a few kids you could tell were loners, so I thought that maybe Jake would hang out with them instead of joining the already formed group of friends that were probably friends from school.

The first day went fine, as we gave the kids a chance to hang out at the park and play some activities, so everyone had a chance to do something they wanted to do. *All right*, I thought, *Things will be fine.*

The next day, we all met at the local swim club in our town. This swim club was a place where teenagers were able to work as lifeguards or as the people that check your cards to make sure you're actually a member. It was open during the summer, and my family used to go to the swim club almost every weekend. Being a spoiled suburban upper-middle class kid, I wanted a pool in the backyard like many of the other kids in my school. We did not have enough room in our backyard for a pool, so my brother, sister, and I would blow up a small pool my mom bought from the store and we would put it on the bottom of the slide to make our own trashy waterpark. We loved it, and then we would go to the pool (my mom would say, "You have a pool! We go to the swim club!") to congregate with the other little kids in what was obviously just a giant toilet.

You can't even imagine the amount of times the employees would get out of the water because a little kid had a "little" accident, which meant they completely defecated themselves in open water. When a kid leaves, frankly, a giant turd in the water, parents should not be allowed to act like the kid had a little "slip" and leaked. No. Absolutely not. Besides, the pool was half water, half urine, and just a lot of chlorine, so many of us kids could have had more diseases than we could possibly understand during a time where things were just much simpler.

So, I gave you that explanation as a major reason why I didn't wear my swimsuit on the days we went to the pool as a camp. The counselors were allowed to swim with their kids, and that sounds almost creepy on paper, but it looks totally fine in real life. When I was kid, I used to put the water I just explained before in my mouth and then spit it out on my brother and sister. Yes, I took the urine and feces touched water into my mouth and spit it out. I think I paid my dues, and I am not going back.

But, I wasn't going to tell the kids all of this because their childhood bliss should not be ruined by the truth of community swimming pools. I was not going to be the bearer of bad news because those counselors are absolutely the worst. It's like a teacher who comes in and only screams at kids and reminds them that they are failures. Very counter-productive, and it would certainly not get me a tip. That's called real priorities.

So, the same boys come back for their second round of bliss. They come one by one, and soon I find Jake leaving his car and literally skipping over to our group. *Ugh, a kid that I would have totally been friends with.* He was also the sweetest kid, and he had the most adorable first grade voice. He was already my favorite of the group, even though that feels unethical, like when mothers say they don't have a favorite kid but they totally do.

Together, the Camp Mafia walked to the table that we would plant ourselves at for the rest of the time. We waited for the swim test, a test every kid has to take before they open the pool, while sitting at the table. Since first graders' patience resembles the size of an ant, they are already running around. Everyone has their bathing suits on, and Jake even has a swim shirt that looks like the one my mother used to put on me because I would get sunburnt on my shoulders (and because I was chubby). But, I chose not to connect with Jake about that one. Apparently, I would soon find out that Jake and I would connect on something else.

As everyone sits down and eats their snack, Jake scurries off to find his backpack, and he fumbles around until he finds something that I made his trademark for the rest of the summer: a magic wand he apparently got from a circus. He takes he out, and it was like time slowed down. The magic wand was pink and had a little veil on it, and many parents would assume it was made for little girls under the age of eight years old. Instead, the real demographic is kids who sweat frequently and wear fitting swim shirts, like Jake and myself. Jake begins running to everyone and sharing his "magic." The other kids don't know how to react, as they have probably never seen anything that "feminine" being held by another boy. We still live in a society that teaches children that boys and girls have separate toys to play with that match both their gender and their "masculine" and "feminine" traits that they are just "magically" born with. It is something that we don't think about very often, but many of us are guilty of doing it. So, it is safe to say the other boys were probably not used to this.

I heard some of the boys giggle, and I saw them looking at Jake. But, I also saw Jake playing with the wand like no one was watching, and it reminded me of my own childhood. I would play with dolls and play with wands like no one was watching, like there wasn't an "issue" to bring up in the first place. There is innocence in children that I sometimes wish I still had. There is a time in everyone's lives where they don't know what is right and what is wrong. They don't know which toys are supposed to be played with by each gender. They don't know that it is not acceptable to urinate in a public pool, and they do it anyway with glee and absolutely no shame.

I thought about the time I brought my doll to school for show and tell. I didn't understand the idea that because I was a boy, it was weird for me to play dolls. I knew that my parents were wary of it, but I didn't understand why. I didn't know what the other kids would think of me because I didn't care. I was excited to be showing off my brand new doll that my mother bought for me at the store. There was no shame that went with it, no strange feelings. I just felt happy.

When Jake first showed off his wand, I thought to myself, *Wow he is brave for doing something like that.* I questioned if he understood what some of the other kids, and even some of the counselors, would think of him. I really thought, *This kid has balls.* But, I realized that this was a child that wasn't "brave" for bringing his wand to camp. That was just the way I thought of it because I am so used to hearing about what kids should and should not be playing with. This first grader did not bring his wand to camp to start a social revolution. Rather, he is an innocent first grader that is blissfully unaware of the social cues that we learn as we grow up.

I have become so used to what is expected of boys and girls that I immediately had thoughts about Jake bringing his wand to camp, to be quite honest. I wasn't thinking that it was wrong for him to bring the wand. Absolutely not. Do you really think the kid who brought both his doll and his calendar to show and tell thinks it's wrong because someone brought in their wand to camp? No. I remember being the only boy who would play with the dolls in the giant dollhouse our teacher brought into school. I did not judge Jake for bringing his wand, but I was worried about the reaction from everyone else.

I wish the world has progressed a bit and we don't have to worry about which toys belong to each gender, but we unfortunately do not live in that world. I don't think we will be able to live in that world for a long time, if ever, because there are too many people focused on proving their "masculinity" to everyone else through the toys they played with, the way they walk, the way they talk, and through the friends they have. Being that person that stood out among the other kids, and not willingly for a long time, I have become used to hearing that boys shouldn't play with dolls. Boys shouldn't talk like that. Boys should be hanging out with other boys. Boys shouldn't have only girl friends. I have become used to hearing how society expects me to act because there apparently is nothing worse than someone being different than everyone else. *God forbid that happens.* Well, good thing I don't believe in God then.

I finally understood why I was so interested in seeing Jake interact with everyone else. It wasn't only because Jake stood out in the crowd, but it was also because I am Jake in so many ways. The major difference between him and I, besides our age, is that he has the innocence that I no longer have. That cannot be controlled, no matter how much many parents probably want that to happen. Jake will eventually lose his innocence too, as it is one of the side effects of becoming older.

I was that boy that brought his doll to school. Then, I learned that boys were not supposed to do that. They would be made fun of for that. They would be called names. They would be considered an outsider. If I knew that when I was in kindergarten, would I have brought my doll into school? I don't know. But, what I do know is that the way society has perceived toys and gender roles in general has been stuck in my head because that has been what I have been taught ever since I was a child. I was taught to be feel bad because I liked dolls instead of basketball. I was taught to not tell anyone that I like to play with dolls because people would make fun of me. Dolls were a girl's toy. And boys playing with toys that belonged to girls was wrong.

Jake didn't know this. He probably still doesn't know this, but I can't be sure. Jake brought his wand to camp, and I immediately had thoughts about it because I have been taught to even slightly question it. I wish I didn't have to think about that, or else maybe I wouldn't be guilty of trying to follow "gender roles" in little ways. I think for the most part, I have been able to do things that would be considered "different" than what other people do. I perform stand-up comedy, where I willingly ridicule myself for a laugh from some of the people that used to call me names. I write about my own insecurities, my wants, and my fears because it is both therapeutic and makes me feel even just a little important in a world that doesn't know who I am. But, I still have fears that have caused me to maybe not do something that I have wanted to do. Can I read my book in public, or is it too "girly?" What would people say if I did this or that? Does the way I speak bother people? Does the way I walk make me prone to insults and humiliation? Listen, I am not that important, and most people don't give a shit about what I do, or at least that is what I like to think.

Jake had a temper that I didn't realize he had until he confronted some of the boys about his wanting to play with the wand. He was defensive, and he was embarrassed that the other kids even questioned his playing with the wand. I could tell this was not the first time someone ahs asked him about it because he was quick to defend himself when he shouldn't have to. It was silly for me to think at the time that he was living in a world completely full of innocence and bliss. You learn social cues and behavior from the people around you and the environment you live in. Lucky for him, he still has enough bliss to push past the questions and probable teasing to keep bringing his wand to camp and playing with it like no one is there. I hope he keeps that. I wish I did, as it took me years to figure out that just because society has an expectation doesn't mean that we have to completely follow them. That's a perk of living in a free country like this one that I take advantage of more and more. But, I have had these expectations lodged in my head so many times as a child that it gets harder to push past them, and it took me a long time to even begin enjoying trying to push past them. I hope Jake does the same, and I hope he doesn't stop playing with his wand because someone tells him boys aren't supposed to do such a thing.

  I also sometimes wish to be a kindergarten child again, blissfully unaware of how the world expects me to act. I wish I could be back in the classroom with the doll, not realizing that some of the other kids would be judging me. But, at the same time, I don't want to be blissfully unaware because I would be able to push past what others think to do what I want to, and sometimes that is more satisfying than not being aware of what is out there at all.

Five Things I Learned My Sophomore Year In High School

So, your freshman year is over, and it is time to celebrate. Being a freshman is only good for so long, and then it just isn't. Not for me, at least. I always wanted to be older than I was, so that just my own issue. But, I am also able to recognize the joys of being a sophomore in high school. And here are some of the things I learned throughout that year.

1. **You are not the youngest anymore, and that is a great thing.**

Congratulations on no longer being a freshman! Sophomores are kind of the middle child of the school, even more so than juniors because juniors get to have upperclassman status. You are no longer being jeered at your school's pep rallies, and you can just feel a little cooler because there is a new class that is one year below you.

2. **The work gets a little easier to manage when you become a sophomore.**

Look, you are not the new kids in school anymore. You are used to the workload you are getting because you are no longer in your transitioning phase. You can either accept that and get your work done or you can not do any of the work because you got senioritis two years early. Up to you! But, the work becomes easier to manage, and personally, I had an easier time with my classes sophomore year than I did my freshman year, but that also depends on your own experience because of the classes you take and what you have going on after school. So, this isn't a universal truth.

3. **Don't worry about college yet. Please.**

I cannot stress this ENOUGH. Do yourself a favor and stop losing your shit as a sophomore. A SOPHOMORE. Oh my God. You have another two years to lose your minds about that. That is why sophomore year is the best year of high school, in my opinion. You are not a freshman anymore, so you are no longer the baby. You don't have to worry about SATs and that load of crap yet because you are not a junior. And, you are not applying to college. Sophomore year is literally the year that represents all of what high school really should be. Do some high school work and not worry about which school you and your friends might go to in two years.

4. Sophomore year is ALWAYS the year high school drama shows begin.

I remember being a kid and fantasizing about what high school would be like by watching melodramatic high school dramas. Coincidentally, they all seemed to have started sophomore year. I have never seen a show that have their characters start their freshman year, except for *Degrassi*, I guess. But, I don't really watch that show at all because that crossed the line for me at too melodramatic, but I'm sure I judged it too soon. Oh, and the actors actually look like high school students, which probably turned me away from the show since every high school I watch have actors that are basically thirty playing students. But, let's be honest, you start off freshman year when you are fourteen years old, and I guess many shows don't want to depict fourteen year-olds having loads of television-perfect sex, heavy drinking, having oddly-adult conversations, doing a lot of drugs at a friend's house, or going out to nightclubs.

According to television shows, that is all supposed to happen when you turn FIFTEEN years old! Let's raise a glass to teenage expectations!

5. It's ok to not know what you want to do you're your life when you are sophomore!

Please don't let people try and convince you to know exactly what you want to do when you are a sophomore. You don't have to know yet because you are not even halfway through high school yet. Just take some time and take classes that interest you so you can see what you want to do. You don't have to know yet, and whatever you are thinking you want to do might change in an instant. Throughout high school, I wanted to be an actor, writer, journalist, screenwriter, director, kind of a screenwriter, comedian, and then a writer/comedian. And my shit is still not together.

All I can say is that enjoy sophomore year for what it is. It is a time where you don't have to worry about college yet, and you can just enjoy the high school experience for whatever you make it out to be. Enjoy it while it lasts, as you will probably appreciate it more once it is over.

The Virgin Diaries

Part One

I am a fifteen-year-old sophomore in high school,
so I should have had sex with at least two guys and I
should have another one on my tail, right? That's at
least what the media tells me. If my life went the way
teenage life is portrayed in television and movies, I
would be having hot sex in a school bathroom right
now instead of writing this essay. But, life doesn't have
the same rules as television and film because there isn't
a screenwriter writing their fantasies and all in your life.
This sounds like a simple thing to understand, but I still
have to remind myself of this because I haven't seemed
to outgrow the idea that my life will work out like the
movies do.

My best friend, Tyler, started dating her first boyfriend during our sophomore year in high school. They met at our school's theater program, a year before I even joined. So, I didn't know him very well until they started seeing each other. What's funny about my relationship with Tyler is that we really do interact like an old married couple that seems like they have been looking at each other for a little too long. That sounds totally cheesy and ludicrous, but we have always worked as a duo. I have a Type-A personality and she mellows me out with a Type-B personality. Tyler is strong-willed and resilient to anything that hits her, while I sometimes take very little things very personally. We both care for and nurture each other when we each need it. We have had little fights, as any friend pairing does, but we have so much love for each other that forms when you are close friends for so many years.

I remember being fourteen years old and picking out different items at the local department store with Tyler for the New York City apartment we would own one day because we would "obviously be roommates." I remember being sixteen and doing the same thing. I remember talking on the phone with her into the late hours of the night until she said "yellow bus" because that was the code word that her parents were coming and she had to go. We used to talk about the kind of guys we wanted to date, and the kind of lives we wanted to leave.

That is why it was so tough for me, personally, when Tyler started dating someone. Ugh, that sounds so terrible selfish, and I hate that. I wish I was that friend that was immediately on board and as supportive as I could be, but I had trouble accepting the fact that my best friend had someone else that would be able to talk to her late at night and have a relationship that was as close as the one I had with her. I was jealous because my friend's attention was on someone else and because I wanted what she had. I wanted someone to be interested in me the way her boyfriend was interested in her, and I also was naïve enough to think that my love life could fall in line with the romantic comedies I believed always came true. Oh, and the other problem was that I thought that fifteen was apparently the year before death.

There is a certain status that teenagers feel they have to achieve before they graduate high school, or at least this is the way I view it: you have to have either dated someone or hooked up with a few people and then throw sex into the equation before you graduate high school. I thought by not having sex by the time you are sixteen years old, you are just not cool enough to hang out with the big boys and girls. How could I not have this mentality? How many teen movies have I seen where everyone is focused on having sex with someone else in some way or another? *American Pie*, *Mean Girls*, and even *Easy A*. The entire plot of *American Pie* was focused on a group of guy friends that vow to lose their virginity by the time they graduate high school. I love that movie and find it hysterical, but it wasn't like they didn't lose their virginity and accepted that. No. They all lost their virginity on the same night and it really only affected one guy that was already in a relationship in the start of the movie. *Mean Girls* had a whole subplot of Caty, the dubbed "good girl" of the film (and with the "good" LiLo, who I miss dearly) trying to get her frenemy Regina's boyfriend for herself. We see Regina in two sex scenes, and there is one where her mother asks if the "kids" want a condom or a snack. Yes, this scene is hilarious, and I laugh at that moment every time I watch the movie, but I didn't realize how much that rang true to some of the parents I see in the area I live in. There is a borderline disturbing complex where many suburban mothers try to act like they are still teenagers, and I have actually seen parents encouraging their teenagers to drink and have sex, and I'm sure they feel that this will make their kids seem "cooler" and make it seem like they have "cooler" parents than the masses. But, I also understand that there is a completely other side to this, as there are parents that just understand that they cannot control what their kids do but are also not trying to act like a friend rather than a parent.

So, it is not always just the teenagers decide what is considered "cool," but there are many parents that add to this overall idea of "coolness." Being gay, I have been told multiple times that college is my "window" of opportunity for a blossoming relationship.

"You're time is coming! But probably in college rather than high school," someone would tell me.

"You just have to wait for the right time!" someone else would share.

When was my time coming? When would I finally get to that point that everyone says I will eventually get to? Not only have I heard that my "time" is my college years, but I have heard that many LGBT people experience what heterosexual teenagers experience involving relationships in their twenties, like being in their first relationship.

Oh my GOD!

It is absolutely horrifying to hear that. There is a part of my teenage years that I haven't even lived yet? And I have to wait for that time to come? I can't even say that they are wrong, but there are always exceptions to this statement. There are enough straight people that don't start dating until after high school and there are enough LGBT people that start dating in high school. It doesn't matter whether I'm straight or gay. I just know that I shouldn't be putting so much pressure on myself. No one should.

Tyler has always told me that I cannot force anything to happen in my love life. You meet someone by coincidence, and it happens from there. Not only am I an impatient person, I also always wanted to be older than I was. I was never content with being a fourteen or fifteen year old young teenager. I always thought I was meant to be in my early twenties, and that would definitely not coincide with my behavior when I was actually fourteen or fifteen. I have had adults tell me that I am an "old soul," and that's only because I put on a good front for adults, as many teenagers do. In reality, I was emotionally a fourteen year old, and I still had a lot of learning to do. So, when Tyler told me that basically waiting was what I had to do, apparently I didn't take that to heart right away because my actions certainly did not show that I was living my life by this mentality.

◆

If you are taller than me, I probably already have a crush on you. I can't help it. I really can't. I am six foot and one inch, and I tend to forget how tall I really am until someone reminds me of that.

"Wow, you are so *tall*," someone would tell me as if they just solved the biggest mystery in the nation.

It is rare that I find someone in my town that is actually taller than me, so I basically have a crush on anyone that fits that criterion. PRIORITIES.

I was a junior in high school, and I was feeling extra desperate than I usually feel in my daily life. I was in gym class, where I was playing a horrific game of volleyball. Gym class is a class I truly hate because it seems to be where the straight guys try to prove who's the strongest of the group. So, that means the victims include everyone else in the class that didn't want to be there in the first place. I have watched too many people get hit in the face by a ball, and I somehow have not yet fallen victim to this kind of tragedy. So, I see the guy I have been eying for the past couple of weeks playing a game of basketball. He was actually on the basketball team, and he was six foot and five inches. He also looked a little shy, which somehow equated to meaning he is gay. My motto in life, which has gotten me nowhere in my romantic life, is as such: Everyone is gay until they prove themselves straight. I wish

I didn't follow my own motto, and I hope other people are smart enough to never do such a thing. Holy straight balls, it is a horrible motto.

In case I have to mention this, I tend to be attracted to straight guys that play sports. Obviously, the perfect place to find a boyfriend for my funny and cute (in my mind) gay self is the sports world. *Are you kidding me?* No, I am of course not generalizing that every person on a sports team is straight. That would completely ruin my image of an athlete falling in love with me. But, it wouldn't be the first place to look when looking for an openly gay student. That shit only happens on shows like *Glee*, or maybe some super progressive high school that I have never seen or heard of in my life. My idea of this happening comes from the films that tell me the kid in a completely different social circle gets to be in a relationship with Chad Michael Murray, who just happens to be on the football team. And no, no one has ever pushed me into a dirty school closet to make out with me after a football game, but I did see that in a film once too. And that happened between two guys. So basically, as much as I love films, I am declaring that they suck.

So, I am trying to play this volleyball game and would quite anything at this point to be able to leave. Luckily, I had one of my friends next to me trying to play the game as well. But, out of the corner of my eye, I see the guy, who I will name Tim in this instance, walk out of the gym to go to the bathroom.

Oh my god, I thought, *this might finally be my moment that I have been waiting for*. Ok, let's break this down and discuss this hot mess of a statement. Let's put this into perspective. I was fifteen years old when I thought this. FIFTEEN God damn it. I wasn't the forty-year-old virgin, and I wasn't going through a "dry spell." There was nothing that happened (or I guess didn't happen) in the first place to constitute the situation as a "dry spell." But, of course, I was acting like I waited the longest time for someone to fall in love with my crazy ass. Oh, and this guy showed absolutely no interest in me. I don't mean we met and then he still wasn't interested. No, he never spoke to me in my life. So, obviously, the place I thought would be the best place for him to fall in love with me was the bathroom.

I obviously didn't think too much about this plan before I executed it, but I thought I really came up with a genius plan within seconds, and I was proud of myself.

"I'll be right back," I declare to my friend who was next to me. She watched as I walked away, and she was two seconds from getting hit in the face with the volleyball and she turns just in time to hit it. *Ugh, such a movie moment. It's all happening.*

I walk out with enough energy to let me walk from New Jersey and California. I was so ready for this. And then I walked into the bathroom.

Let me break down the scene of the crime: two stalls, two sinks, two urinals, and the victim peeing in one of the urinals.

What the hell was I thinking, I thought.

The energy I had went from my feet to my stomach, where I felt like I wanted to throw up. But, I had some energy left in my feet to keep me going. I couldn't leave at that point. That would have been weird, which I apparently I am able to say based on my own actions. I didn't even pretend to have to pee, which would have been a half-smart decision. No, I went right towards the sink and started washing my hands. Do you know that super uncomfortable eye contact between two people when one is washing their hands and the other one is peeing? No? Me neither. But it happened. And it was my fault. We made the awkward eye contact, and I was caught between a rock and a urinal. So, I decided to say what I thought was the most appropriate things to say.

"I'm not in here for no reason," I declared, like a spy who was doing a terrible job at his work.

What resulted from that was a giggle from Tim, but it was the kind of giggle you would give someone that is holding you hostage and decided to make a "funny" to pass the time. Or, just a usual time at your grandparents' house.

"Totally fine," he muttered.

Ugh, this was the moment! He fell in love with me just from my charming bathroom habits.

"And please don't hit me when we play pin-ball!" I confidently say, "It is horrifying."

Background: Pinball is a game that we played in gym class that was basically dodgeball but with pins you had to hit as well. It is a game that tests both your physical and mental strength, and I probably failed at both.

"Haha, no problem man," He politely responds.

Is man a term that straight guys use a declaration that you are in the friend zone? Probably. I didn't know this yet. I thought it was an affectionate term.

He left the bathroom after our thrilling and insightful conversation, and I stayed in the bathroom for an extra minute to reflect on what I just did. I just walked in to the bathroom to try and flirt with a guy who was peeing at the same time. And the only thing I could mutter was "I am not in here for no reason."

But, I walked back into the gym with way too much confidence. I thought I made a friend that day in the bathroom, a possible but not probably high school boyfriend. In reality, I probably scared him, and we only talked a few times after that. Poor guy.

As I said before, I am an inpatient person. I am fifteen years old, and I want to fall in love. I want someone to want to be with me. I want someone to want to talk to me. To hold me. To love me. I want what my best friend has, and I wish I wasn't so jealous. I thought Tim could be the "one" in high school that everyone seems to have in the movies. But, as Tyler always said, you can't force anything to happen. Meeting someone is by coincidence. The idea that I could tamper with "coincidence" by acting like meeting someone in the bathroom is perfectly natural and coincidental is ridiculous, and I even knew that at the moment just a little, but it didn't stop me.

I feel the pressure to have to find love immediately. High schoolers, especially the ones that are single, act like not finding someone at the age of fifteen means you are basically the forty-year-old virgin. In reality, love is not about age. It's about emotional stability and liking yourself before anyone can actually love you. I wish I knew when I was fifteen that I didn't mean to have sex with someone to feel worthy of myself. I need to think that to myself even now in the present day.

But, I had so much to learn that I didn't even know yet, and I still have so much to learn. All I know is that I am fifteen years old, and I have to like myself above all else. I can't rely on a guy to tell me this, or rely on him to cover up my own insecurities. Oh, did I have so much to learn.

Update:

First lesson to learn: I wrote about bathroom-gate for a screenplay that I handed in to a teacher. She wrote back,

"This was on the line of being funny or creepy. Thank goodness it was funny!"

And that is the moment where I realized that my "romantic pursuits" could be equated to glorified stalking. Oh, so much to learn.

Five Things I Learned My Junior Year In High School

Junior year. *Oh my God!* That is the only way to describe junior year. What's funny about junior year is that everyone told me that it is a terrible year and I will not get enjoyment out of it. They make it sound like the most terrible year of all, and I don't remember getting any words of support before I started from anyone that has been through it before. Sometimes, I do the same thing. I tell people how bad it is because junior year is the kind of years that binds people of all ages together in its awfulness. It reminds us that we are getting older, and it gives us a "power" over the underclassmen that don't understand the work that has to be done that year. So, we are compelled to talk about how bad it is to the ones that don't know. But, in reality, junior year was tough, but it was also one of the fastest years for me. I think the amount of work we had made the time move along, and I can genuinely say that I enjoyed myself in different aspects of the entire year. It was the most challenging year of high school for me because of the pressure that came along with it, but here is what I learned during that year:

1. Stop losing your shit over the SATs.

Oh my god, calm down. Please. Everything will be fine. This is a phrase that people don't tell enough juniors or the overambitious underclassmen before they take the SATs. EVERYTHING WILL BE FINE. The SATs suck, and they will always suck, but your score is your score. I was lucky enough to have a tutor, and I know so many people can't even afford to take a class, but your score can either improve or not. A tutor helped me study and learn things I apparently needed to know for the test, but I actually had to work in the book and study that way to even focus for the test. I took the SATs twice, and then I took the ACTs twice, and I went with my ACT score rather than my SAT score and I had a tutor specifically for my SAT. So, sometimes a class or a tutor may not change anything drastically, as I just naturally did better on the ACT without a tutor's guidance. But, there are so many more things to focus on than just standardized testing. Here's an idea: just work hard in school and get the best grades you can there. Do some activities that you like to do that can make your hardest school day just a little better. And don't let standardized tests take over your life. It's just not worth it.

2. College visits are not everything.

Ok, this sounds a little strange because people have been telling you that college is everything your junior year of high school. It isn't. It is good to start figuring out which schools to visit and eventually apply to next year, but there is still a barrier between your junior year and college that is called senior year. I got more out of college visits my senior year than my junior year because I knew it was happening in only a year. There are still so many things to learn junior year, and you never know what you will totally want by the time you apply to college. Junior year, I wanted to go to college in Los Angeles, and that was basically where my top schools were. Now, my top school is in New York City, and that changed in the course of one year. Things change, and sometimes you want something else, and that is perfectly fine.

3. You are finally upperclassmen, sort-of.

Yes, you are upperclassmen now, and that is all well and good. You finally don't feel like the little fish in the school anymore. But, both sophomore and junior year are like the middle children of the entire school.

They exist, but they may not get as much attention as the youngest kids and the oldest kids. For some, this is bliss. No one is trying to remind you that you are the youngest kid so you have so much to learn and no one is reminding you that you are leaving in a few months. So, you are an older group in the school, but you are not the *oldest* yet. But, you still have a prom, which is basically the symbol of being an older group in the school.

4. **Telling people how much junior year sucks/is going to suck only gives you temporary pleasure.**

Yes, junior year is not the best year in high school. Everyone who goes to high school knows this. But, telling every living underclassman how much it is going to suck only makes you feel good for about two slightly wonderful minutes. As people, we like to make others feel bad when we are down, and we can all pretend that we are not those assholes that do. No, we are all those assholes sometimes. So, in your most stressful of times during your junior year, you might tell someone who is younger how terrible it will be for them. It is worth it for the two minutes, but you will just go back to hating the year again and feeling miserable. I learned from experience that the highest you go from telling someone that is probably equivalent to the height of the Starbucks building go to every day to try and survive the year.

5. Try and enjoy the good parts of the year. It makes it go by faster.

You want the year to go by faster? My response: try and find the good things about junior year and run with that. You might be on the varsity team for whatever sport you are throwing balls in. You might be part of the older group in your theater program, so you have more experience hysterically crying on demand (I am still working on that). You might have spent more time in whatever club you are in. You will get your driver's license this year (unless you are too young or was just lazy with getting your permit in your sophomore year). You have your prom this year, so it's a step up from the probably horrific eighth grade dance you had a few years ago. Enjoy the little things, and your year will hopefully be a little better and smoother.

Junior year will not last forever, and that's a wonderful thing. Before you know it, the year is over. And then you will be a senior, and that's a whole other horse you will have to ride in the high school rodeo. It's a tough year, but it is manageable. Even the ones who talk about how terrible it is/will be survive, no matter how much they make it seem like they wouldn't. We all survive it because it is a year that isn't meant to literally kill somebody. Just sit down, work hard, and try to enjoy the ride.

Behind the Chat Rooms

During one summer night, when I would usually be watching reality television or binge eating some potato salad from the supermarket, I decided to enter a chat room for the first time since I was in middle school. I am recalling the very few times in middle school that I would enter a chat room, and the experiences never turned out to be entirely a pleasant one. You find the same kind of people in chat rooms: the "sixteen" year old that is really forty, the online masturbators, some foreign people with predator mustaches, and the sick curious kids like myself that decide to enter the party. At times, chat rooms feel like a fucked up United Nations gathering.

When I was a mere twelve-year-old LAD (loser and desperate), I entered the chat rooms with a few friends at the local library after school. We had a few lovely conversations with some people from India, some conversations with "teenagers" that ended with them ending the chat when we started to try and be funny, and some grown adults that admitted that they didn't have a job and they sat around on chat rooms all day. When we got home, it was go time. We had our computer set up, and we turned the video camera on. Since I was a paranoid child (and I continue to be probably the most paranoid person in the room), I insisted on covering our faces with our hand or a pillow so we could only see the person and they wouldn't be able to see us BECAUSE if someone were to come to my house and kidnap someone, their first choice would be a too-tall-for-middle-school boy that listens to radio pop hits (still guilty of this).

My friends and I found that video chatting with strangers was not that fulfilling. All we found were snotty teenage girls that started laughing when they heard me speak and grown men that had their computer facing their chicken neck so we could watch them choke it. It was like watching porn but with a bad filmmaking style and eerie dark lighting. That was another thing that was weird about the video chats: everyone's lights seemed to be off as my friends and I had the lights on in my parent's office with suburbia taking up the background. Our friends from wherever all looked like they made a home for themselves in a hole in the ground.

After spending a short period of time letting our middle school brains being scarred by old men's overripe bananas, we retired from visiting chat rooms. Oh, and I was always nervous that my parents would yell at me for going on chat rooms. My parents tried to scare me by telling me that people could look up our IP Address and kidnap me in my own home, and this was also their logic when telling us why not to watch porn. Parenting tactic: scare kids into thinking porn is the gateway to kidnapping. Kids' hormones can only handle so much adversity before finally giving in to fear and un-sexiness.

One fateful (extremely boring) night in high school, my friend and I decided to make our return to the chat room that once showed my middle school mind what an uncircumcised penis looked like, and I most definitely did not like what I saw. This time, we decided to turn on the video chat. Being paranoid (some things never change once you leave middle school), we still covered our faces with a pillow. Actually, the only thing that was actually visible was my friend's cleavage. My face was naturally covered, as I didn't want to ruin the sexual mood that some video chatter-ers have by showing my face when being smushed by a pillow. The experience consisted of many men telling my friend that she had a "nice rack" and I had an annoying voice. At one point, I even started asking people if my voice was annoying right when we were connected to a new person to chat with. The answers ranged from extreme statements like "fuck yes" to extreme actions like immediately ending the video chat. Obviously, some people do not know proper video chat etiquette. And for saying this statement right here, someone would have hung up on me.

So, the night wasn't very successful besides having a story to shamelessly tell people later. But, that night would not be the only time I re-emerged on a chat room. That was only the beginning of my venture to the world of creepy perverts and curious teenagers.

◆

Over the summer, I randomly decided to enter a gay chat room for the first time. My research did not go far, as a quick search for "gay chat room" can lead you to many chat rooms with clever names that gay men came up with during a lunch meeting.

I had one of those fits where I was upset about being single and decided that I was going to "change my life" (re. dramatic child). I fell upon one of the first chat rooms in my search, and I found in each chat room that I fell into had both a major chat room with every user on there and a separate chat box to talk to one specific user. On the side bar, the "polite" thing to do is to write your age, gender, and apparently what your sexual orientation is. Sometimes, if you want to be brutally honest, you can announce whether you like to be on the top or the bottom of both your virtual and actual sex. I decided to keep it very simple and write down "m/g/17," which stands for male, gay, and seventeen years old. I looked for people that claimed to be seventeen years old as well, and I clicked some of their usernames to start a private chat with them.

The first name I feel upon on was a guy that has the username "m/17," and I already decided it was the perfect and "safest" candidate in the strange chat room dating pool.

I didn't want to come off too strong immediately, as I already got a few messages from some overzealous men that started the conversation with, "Do you want to have video chat sex?" And I am writing the censored version of what some of those messages actually said. Basically, it seemed like the perfect message to find any horny person to video chat with them is, "Hey, can I _(enter dirty sex act)_____ to your __(any body part with some sort of hole in it- I have heard it all)_____ over video chat?" Comforting. Safe. Healthy. Three words you may never see in a chat room but I am using now to describe the obviously comforting, safe, and healthy situation. So, instead, I decided to show everyone that I am a baby to the world of cyber-hyper-sexuality by writing, "Hey," to the first chat. Responding in enthusiasm, m/17 responded with a mere, "sup." It was love at first sight. And I could tell because the conversation was extremely boring.

From the top of my head, I can remember that we were talking about where he lived and what he was doing.

"Eating food," he wrote, as I was lying in my bed with the urge to make myself some cinnamon buns.

By the end of our conversation, he told me that he wasn't gay at all. No. And, he wasn't bisexual. NOPE. He was a straight guy who came on to this specifically LGBT chat room out of straight-guy-curiosity. ARE YOU FUCKING KIDDING ME? To me, this is hilariously ironic. The amount of straight guys I have liked and thought could fall in love with me just by greeting me is just a little ridiculous. No, when I make the effort to plant myself in a chat room designated for LGBT people, specifically gay and bisexual men, the first guy I talk to randomly happens to be a straight guy. The conversation ended quickly, as I told him that I am actually gay and for once the straight guy is the minority in the room. He wasn't too fond of that statement, and left. I assume he realized that his curiosity was a little weird (as if I have the right to tell people that their actions are weird), and he logged out of the chat room.

My next conquest (more like prospect) was a guy that came unexpectedly in my life, as he clicked on my username and started the chat with me first. He wrote to me that he was five feet tall and was looking for someone to "give him height." No. Bye.

I clicked on someone else's username and said, "Hey," to them and our conversation ended up consisting of friendly greeting that you would think is innocent until it isn't anymore. Those gay men are sneaky as hell in their chat rooms because they are nice until they attack you with weird requests of sexual activity. Here is an example of a conversation I had with someone:

Me: Hey

User: Hey

Me: What's up?

User: Nothing, how about you?

Me: Nothing. Just came on this chat room for the first time and checking it out. Have you been on here before?

(This was my version of the very dumb, "Have you been to this bar before?" that lots of men ask women when the men have obviously been there many times and keep coming back looking for another date for the night. I have now virtual-fied it and made it 2015 friendly. Progress!)

User: Yes

(This is where the two-minute pause comes in because I have no idea how to respond to someone that gives you absolutely nothing to work with. But, I probably would think I have them hooked just from one-word answers. I don't.)

User: I want to fuck you now so let's video chat.

WHAT?! What the hell is this?! I have never been more flattered and disgusted in my life. All I did was say hello to someone online and they now want to virtually have sex with me? I didn't even bring out the cheesy jokes yet. But, how many guys has this guy been asking this question to all day? So, I am not feeling very special anymore. Who knew an ulterior motive of mine was to enter a chat room and feel special? (Re. So much to learn. So much.)

But, regardless, I have had a few chats where it turns from innocent boring small talk to immediately grabbing the penis by its horns and asking you to take it for them. These offers were bold, in your face, and frank, so basically the offers represented an actual penis. I am horrified.

I left the conversation after that, with the same excuse I gave some of the other offers, "Sorry, my camera isn't working!" The suitors don't stay after that. No way.

They are out faster than my mother's wine bottle from the fridge after a long day of work.

So, I decided to try and weed some of the users out of my chat pool by writing in the designated and overwhelming chat where each user can write in. In the biggest font, you could see of the users writing what kind of user they want to chat with and their requests to follow. I decided to be less overwhelming and write in a cuter and more innocent medium font, and the words I wrote are as follows:

IF YOU ARE SIX FEET TALL OR TALLER, CHAT ME.

That's right, I was keeping it real and totally honest. If some of these crazies were trying to find guys that could put their legs behind their heads at the ripe age of fifty and older, I think I could ask for someone that was over six feet tall. Personally, I am six foot and one inch tall, and it is a challenge to find someone that is either my height or a little shorter or a little taller, but I apparently I like to make things a little harder for myself because I have accepted that challenge. I haven't been five feet and eight inches tall since before I had a "1" in front of my age, and I am not going back to Kansas now.

The promotional advertisement of my personal self did not go as well as I expected, and I did not expect much from my frank offer. To be specific, the highlight of my offer was someone asking to be my "slave." Here is the conversation, according to my possibly faulty memory since it was not a pleasant one.

User: Do you want to be my slave-owner and I'll be the slave?

Me: Do you ask that to everyone you talk to?

User: Kinda.

Me: Does it work?

User: Yeah, haha. So, do you want to?

Me: That is a lovely offer, but no thank you. Good luck finding what you want, though.

User: Thanks.

Ok, so I might have condensed that conversation and fixed the grammar a bit. But, I remember him asking me that and me deciding to screw around with him because I was bored and shocked that he would ask something so offensive and strange. I also remember politely declining the invitation and wishing him luck. So, this is the version of the conversation I have for you.

But, I did have a chance to start talking to a guy from London who claimed to be six feet and five inches and also claimed to be seventeen years old. I probably peed myself a little when I saw this user in the box of chats. He began chatting with me first, as he must have saw my advertisement next to the one from the old man that offered to be someone's "daddy" right above. We had a fun conversation, but I had to remind myself that he lived in London so whatever I could imagine happening with our "forming relationship" would actually never happen. Oh, and he said he would be right back and then never came back at all. So, I guess my London lover is gone, and I will keep waiting for his return.

I then began talking to another possible cyber-suitor, and he said that he was nineteen years old that went to college in New York City. Holy shit balls, was this a moment. We had a nice conversation, and I thought he was super funny and charming (as charming as one could be in a online chat room designed for hook-ups and bored teenagers), and Cinderella and her prince's night was interrupting by a clock striking midnight in the form of a text message from my younger sister.

"Hey Brandon, can you pick me up at my friend's house now?" the stepmother growled.

I had to leave the chat temporarily so I could fulfill my destiny of being a chauffer for my sister, but I left one slipper for the NYC prince by telling him I would be right back and I would leave my computer open to the chat would stay running. So, I left to pick up my sister, and I returned to my chat and sent a message to my "suitor" and awaited his return. What else could I have been doing during this hot summer day? Well, I came home from my summer job at noon, and apparently I had nothing better to do than cyber hunt for cyber men. I thought it was working this time. Emphasis on the words, "I thought," because he didn't respond. I even left my computer open for an hour as I did other things, and the prince never returned. Thus, Cinderella was left in the cyber castle that smelled like sweat and desperation, and I was fueling the energy by my own obvious desperation for attention.

On the last leg of my chat room tour, I started talking to a guy that claimed to be bi-sexual and nineteen years old. Ok, I'll take it. We are chatting about how he goes to college in Florida, and it started off as innocent small talk. So, of course, I thought it would soon turn into a tainted conversation because the user would ask if I wanted to video chat and change the entire game, to which I would decline and then leave the chat every single time. But, the chat turned into one that was unexpected for me to see, and I am surprised I didn't think that something like this could happen.

He told me he was bi-sexual, but he asked me to keep it a secret because no one knew about his sexuality. I could tell he had his guard up, as I have always had since you never know who you can really trust on the internet, and I told him that I would keep his secret. Who would tell about his sexuality? I didn't know him, and I didn't even know his name. We have never met before, and we live in two different states with quite a distance between them. But, there was desperation to not have people know about his sexuality, even on an anonymous online forum. He told me his parents would not accept him for who he is, and even his friends do not know that he is bi-sexual.

It was definitely a change from the usual conversations, as you can't find anything more different than an overly confident gay and a scared and timid bi-sexual. I felt terrible for him, and I wasn't sure how to help him. I told him that the people that truly love and care for him would be the ones that stay with him and accept him when he comes out to them. He did not know when he would want to tell his parents, but he was scared that they would leave him like he was never really their kid at all. I have been lucky because I was able to come out to my parents at fourteen years old and they accept me for who I am, and I cannot imagine not being able to tell my parents and my friends something as, in all seriousness, something as simple as who I am attracted to. We tend to make coming out bigger than it needs to be because we have been taught that coming out is something that has to be a big deal when it really should not be. But, I realize this is coming from the guy that was lucky enough to have his parents accept him when there are so many LGBT youth that struggle because their parents, friends, and other loved ones will not accept them for who they are.

The user and I eventually stopped talking, but I never forgot the conversation we had together. It's both funny and sad to think about the pool of people in one chat room. You have one person who is confident in his sexuality and you have another person right above the other one in the chat box that is scared to be who they are in his real life so they turned on a computer to see what or who is out there that can relate to them. We like to show our best selves on the internet, and I am entirely guilty of doing this. When you look at my tweets, you can see that I tend to only tweet silly jokes and self-promotion bullshit that only represents a small portion of my actual life. I have never been the one to "subtweet," and to tweet my deepest and personal feelings that I am afraid to even share with my closest friends. Even on chat rooms, I am able to make myself look like a confident person looking for some "fun" online, when that is not true to my real personality. I was never able to (and still not able to sometimes) talk to some of the guys with confidence in real life the way I have done online because I don't have the safety blanket of being on a LGBT designated chat room in real life.

Hiding behind a computer makes saying things so much easier than saying it to someone's actual face. Being flirty is much easier to do online when you cannot see if someone is actually responding well to it or if they are giving you a disgusted look that one would make if you were talking to someone that didn't brush their teeth that morning. Hiding behind a computer makes it easier to share your feelings to a stranger that you would never meet, but it doesn't make it totally easier to share your emotions to your "virtual friends" that go to the same high school as you do.

After I finished chatting with the user from Florida, I closed the chat room for the final time, and I have not returned since. I realized, among other things, that chat rooms were not the appropriate place to find possible dates, for more reasons than one. I also realized how chat rooms are a cesspool of many people are looking for many things and are desperately searching for them. Whether you are a confident gay man who wants someone to video chat with because they are bored and horny, or someone that is looking to escape their marriage and live their fantasies on online chat rooms, or someone that is looking for a safe place to hide from the hell they have to call their home, everyone is looking for something. What the hell am I doing? I am looking for some sort of love in the wrong place. I am looking for the comfort of someone giving me romantic attention, whether it is through someone holding my hand to my hand holding the mouse that guides our silly online chat. And even in the most unexpected places, I realize during times that I forget it because I am consumed in my ridiculous teenage life, I am one of the lucky ones.

Stand the F**k Up:

The First Time I Took Control of the Way I Perceived Myself

My bed was the hub of watching comedians making fun of everything from social class to celebrity culture. My bed was the hub of watching the ones who claim they were never the "cool" kids back in the day become the ones that make other laugh and pay for a ticket to see someone stand on a stage with a microphone and make jokes. They were the "cool" ones now, and I thought that was so cool. The best comedians have their audience in their control, and they could make them laugh with just a few words, if I am correct in my reasoning.

My bed was the first place where I started watching comedians like Kathy Griffin, who always claimed to be the girl in school that had to ward bullies away from her by making them laugh. Now, she jokes about being a "D-lister" in a world with the seemingly perfect celebrities that live an insane lifestyle. Meanwhile, I am laying on my bed in my pajamas fawning over the life she has created for herself. This is someone who decided that, instead of letting people beat her, she decided to be the one that made fun of herself. I have always admired that she, as well as many other comedians was able to make the joke about herself before someone else could do it. She took control over the way she perceived herself, and I have always wanted to do something that "cool."

I have heard many times that stand-up comedians do what they do because they want to feel important and feel gratified, and laughing is one of the easiest ways to tell if someone is enjoying what you are telling them. I have always admired stand-up comedians, but I did not start performing stand-up comedy until the middle of my junior year in high school. I saw an email for a talent night that my school was hosting by the choir teacher, and I randomly asked my friend if I should do it. With a weary and confused "ok," I decided to go to auditions a few days later.

I don't remember exactly why I decided to do stand-up at the moment, but I knew it was something that I wanted to try. But, I had absolutely no experience in the "art." Well, you never really have experience until you go on stage and try it, but it wasn't like I was sitting at home writing possible comedy acts for my future attempts at performing. I was completely empty-handed, and all I carried with me was some possible ideas from stories I thought were funny.

I finished and prepared my first comedy set the day before auditions occurred. Truthfully, I should have been finished earlier considering it was my first stand-up performance, but I was feeling a mix of confidence and fear over the possible performance. There weren't many stand-up comedians to my knowledge that went to my high school. I remember one guy that performed a couple of times during the talent nights, but he wasn't very popular with the crowd.

My finalized set list is as follows:

1. Story about me trying to flirt with a guy in the bathroom.
2. Calling out high schoolers for their amazingly annoying Instagram habits (I referenced a favorite I like to call a "toilet selfie," which is where someone takes a photo of themselves or someone else while they are on the toilet.
3. Trying to talk to some guy after auditioning for the talent night that ended up being a bad experience that involved me tripping after I told my brother's friends (waiting outside while I tried getting the other guy's attention), "I do comedy."

I wanted to have my act involve things that other high schoolers could relate to, and the crowd loved the act.

Looking back on it, I wonder whether they really liked the act itself or if they liked it because there are no other stand-up comedians (or very few of them) in the small town that I live in. I wonder what would happen if I took my set to a comedy club. Would they actually like it or would they totally boo me and then say my set is a bunch of high school problems? Or, in more frank terms, it just totally sucks?

The biggest compliment/insult I have received from people that have seen my act is if I stole it from a professional comedian and performed it. Ok, two responses. One: the fact that someone thinks my act is from a professional comedian is both amazing and frightening because I spent little time writing the first act, which is a fault on my part as an aspiring performer. Two: Am I not smart enough to write my own funny act for an audience? Well, I wore a white and blue sweater with very white jeans with some sneakers for my first performance, and I could have looked like a Hispanic shooting star because of the lighting. So, you make that decision for yourself.

To be honest, I thought I was kind of hot shit for a while after my first performance. I really did, and I am not proud of it. I don't think I showed it off that much to the public, but I started to think of myself as an almost professional comedian after ONE performance. That sounds so terrible, but I'll own it. I finally thought that I was able to make fun of myself and make others laugh instead of always being afraid that people were going to laugh at me. Honestly, the "if you can't beat them, join them" sounds a little screwed up if you are talking about making fun of yourself, but our society seems to accept that mentality if you are a comedian performing on stage, and I have definitely accepted that mentality as well.

Thinking I was hot shit, I decided to sign up for my second performance a few months later, and it was at an all-night fundraiser that occurs every year in different areas across the country. The committee emailed the student body and asked us if any of us wanted to perform, and I immediately thought it would be a "fun" experience if I could sign up and perform. My best friend, Tyler, immediately told me that it may not be the best idea, and she had a valid point. This was an outdoor charity event that consisted of team members staying up all night with a least one team member from each group walking around the track. Oh, and I was performing at midnight. So, it wasn't exactly the prime time to perform stand-up. Basically, if I wanted to succeed, I would need to have a good set. I wish I knew this before I hopped up on stage.

Ok, I am not saying it was a terrible performance. But, out of the four shows I have performed, it was probably my worst performance. The set consisted of me making fun of a prom that didn't happen yet, me talking about television shows that aired years ago that no one in the audience obviously watched, and God knows what else I was talking about. The audience responded well to a few jokes, and I am pretty sure one of those jokes was a dirty joke, which is always appropriate during a charity event supporting cancer research with little children around.

I thought I was hot shit when I walked into the event, and I left feeling chilled. It was my own fault. I had different ideas for what my act could be, and I wrote the ideas down on my phone between January and May. But, I didn't totally have a solid plan for what I was going to say. At one point during the performance, I checked my phone to see if I "had anything else to say." So, there you have that. Another issue was that I had stories to tell without solid jokes. I decided that would be alright because I came up with some jokes on the spot during my first performance, and I thought I could do the same thing during the charity performance. DON'T DO THAT.

I got a mixed response from the performance that night. For the people that have never seen me perform before, I got a lot of positive reception, but my friends knew that it was not my best one. Even when some people give me compliments about that performance to this day, I can't help but cringe a little. And, that I felt like the power I once had to make fun of myself before someone else could do it was taken away. Actually, what made it worse was that I felt that I threw the power away, and I wanted it back.

So, the next performance I had was for a charity event that my friend hosted. I created the set with actual jokes in place, and I finally felt like I had my shit together (or as together as it can be) for this performance. It went well, and I consider it to be my best performance to date. And, I felt like I took the power that I had and lost back again.

◆

One might think that it is childish to look at stand-up comedy as a tool for gaining "power," if it even exists in the situation. They are right. It totally is childish. I shouldn't be thinking about the idea of power and, in a way, trying to make up for the years that people have laughed at me behind my back. I shouldn't be trying to change an inevitable situation: some people are just not nice. But, I am guilty of trying to change the way people perceive me. We do this all the time, as I have come to realize. We do this through our work, the people we are friends with, the people we choose to socialize with outside of our friends. We are always trying to find a way to make our image better because even the biggest asshole does not want to always be known as a giant asshole.

They say comedians become comedians because they have the need to feel wanted and loved, since "so many of them" were bullied when they were kids. Or they were considered the "weird ones." They say that writers write about their fantasies and the life they wish they had but would never lead.

I started performing stand-up comedy because I wanted to change the way I perceived myself. I wanted to change the way people perceived me. Everyone likes someone who is funny. Everyone likes someone that can help them escape their own troubles by making them laugh at troubles they may or may not be facing. Comedy is a form of escape for myself because it makes me feel bigger than I really am. It makes me feel more important than I actually am. It makes me feel like I am somebody that isn't the person that just watches videos of comedians in his bed with his pajamas on and a bag of pretzels on the side.

I began writing because it was a form of escape for me. I could write about anything I wanted. I could write about the life I wish I had but wasn't living. I could write about the struggles of my day, and I could write about how what I am writing about is something I couldn't tell anyone else but the paper and the pen.

Damn right, I am looking for gratitude, but I am not entirely proud of that. It is always nice when people appreciate and enjoy what you do. I love writing, and I love comedy. I love performing on stage and making people laugh. I hate having the middle school mentality that I have to laugh at myself before someone laughs at me. Even finishing high school, I am not completely able to get over that. I am still scared of what people will say about me, no matter how much I try to pretend not to care.

One thing I can say, no matter what my intentions are for performing, is that I have learned to laugh at myself more by performing stand-up. I have learned not to take myself too seriously, and I have learned to laugh a little more instead of letting little comments get to me all the time. I used to be the sensitive child that cried whenever someone would say something a little "mean," and now I rely on laughs by making fun of myself. I love that I can do that now.

I want someone in the audience to be able to relate to me because they are going through what I went through. I want that person to know that they are not alone. I want that person to know that it is ok to make mistakes. It is ok to be a human and laugh at what we put ourselves through every day. I want them to know that not everyone is laughing at them, even when he or she thinks they are. I perform for selfish reasons, of course, but I also perform to get through that person. To get through to the ones that feel they have to live up to certain expectations so people will like them more. To the ones who are afraid to be truly human.

Five Things I Learned Senior Year In High School

This is the END. No, but really, people make it sound like this is the end of our entire lives. It's isn't. BUT, it is a year full of goodbyes, and it is the year before the biggest change of our lives so far. So, here are a few things I have learned during this year of high school:

1. Senior year does not end when it begins.
You don't have to cry on your first day of senior year. It just began. You still have 179 other days before the crying happens and the real goodbye comes. There are

many things to celebrate before you leave high school, and letting crying take over actually enjoying your time will just make you feel miserable.

2. It's totally fine to not know where you are going to college yet (if you choose to go to college).
Everyone acts like we should know exactly where we are going to college once we graduate by the time senior year starts. That logic does not make total sense because we apply to multiple schools and ultimately choose one from there. Should you have an idea of which schools you like? Sure. You are beginning the college application process, and it would most definitely help if you knew which schools you want to apply to. But, you do not have to know which school you are most definitely going to in the beginning of the year. Save that mess for the late winter and spring.

3. Being eighteen has its perks to a degree.
Turning eighteen is super exciting because you can finally say you're an adult and mean it when you fight with your parents and say, "I'm basically an adult!" when you are actually fifteen years old. But, really? We are living in our parents' house and living off of their food and board. So, we are about as adult as our dog that happens to be forty-nine in dog years but still cannot understand the concept that people in the outside world are not trying to attack and kill our family.

4. You're never told old for a movie night with friends.

People make senior year out to be the year where you have to attend all of these parties because everyone is together for "one last time." First of all, not freakin' true. See you on Thanksgiving where you give thanks by puking up cheap beer. It's alright to want to have a little movie night with friends with some Chinese food and sweatpants. If you have never done that (which I have trouble believing), then do yourself a favor and do. Too many people in high school drink like alcoholics anyway, so I'm sure the beer will be there again next weekend.

5. Classes still mean something, no matter how much we don't want to admit that.

I know we all like to pretend that being accepted to college means that we can fail all of our classes without consequences. I hate being that asshole, but your "dream" college will still see the rest of your grades for the remainder of the year. Don't stress yourself out so much like you probably did in your junior year. That's not necessary. But, don't allow yourself to completely fail the class after doing well the first half of the year. That's not necessary, either.

Yes, senior year is full of goodbyes. But, it is also opens the door to a new chapter in your life. I remember being that kid who wished that I was in college by the end of the end of my freshman year. Truthfully, I wish I appreciated high school more than I did. High school can be tough, as any time in your life can be, but it is also the place where I both physically and mentally grew, and I am happy to say that I am not totally the same person that I was when I walked into the front doors for the first day of my freshman year.

Don't get me wrong. I am excited for college, and I think I am not only speaking for myself when I say that most seniors want to go to college when they begin their senior year of high school. But, this is also the time where I realized that letting go of high school, the place I have been used to being in for four years, is harder than I thought it would be when I was a whining freshman that thought I was better than this school.

Now, I realize that maybe I am not ready to totally say goodbye, but I don't have the choice to do so. Ultimately, leaving high school is inevitable, as is change. That is why senior year became the year I had to start accepting change more than I ever had to before.

The Virgin Diaries

Part Two

I am an eighteen-year-old virgin, and I absolutely hate it. I told my best friend, Tyler, the other day on the train that I have felt my only relationship experiences have been through what I have seen, rather than what I have actually done. I have watched my parents, I have watched television shows and movies where two people fall in love just by looking at each other, and I have watched my best friend's relationship. I have seen other people form relationships, and all I have really done is make uncomfortable conversation that one might call "bad flirting" in the bathroom.

Physically, I am an eighteen-year-old "adult." Romantically, I stand at a good twelve-years-old. I hear every day the stories of the hook ups at parties, and I have heard of all the relationships make ups and break ups and all of the nuts and bolts that seem to make a relationship work. There are times where I have felt that is enough for me to totally understand what relationships are and "how to have one." In reality, that is about as true as me being an Asian female.

I don't know if it is the idea of relationship that makes me want one so badly. Or, maybe it is the idea of having someone want you physically and emotionally. I have always wanted that, but I know it is has not always been for the "right reasons." I remember wanting one because I want someone to fill the hole that I felt I could not fill myself. I wanted someone to make me feel good about myself in times when I feel down. I wanted someone to tell me that there was not anything wrong with me. I wanted someone to tell me that I am worthy of love because the person who loves me is right there next to me.

I watched a show where a guy, who was thirty, was fighting with his boyfriend about their relationship. They first began an affair, and then they began officially dating once his boyfriend broke up with the ex he was cheating on. At its peak, the guy talks about how he wanted a relationship because he wanted to prove to himself and his loved ones that he was capable and worthy of being in love and being in an relationship. It was one of the more startlingly honest portrayals of a relationship that I have seen on any television show or movie, and it held up a mirror to my own face, even though I am not in a relationship. What makes me want to be in a relationship so badly? What am I trying to prove?

I am trying to prove to myself that I am not going to be a forty-year-old virgin, which is an actual fear of mine. There are days where I am very confident and feel that I can take over the world and have any person fall in love with me, and there are days where I want to hide in the corner. Even on the best days, I have to remind myself that not every person I talk to has the possibility of liking me, whether that is because they are not gay or bisexual or because they are just not attracted to me.

Even though it is a childlike mentality, I still have little fears of being picked on because I "flirted" with the wrong person. *What if he and his friends make fun of me because I tried to have a conversation with him?* I am in the beginning of my adult years, and I still sometimes live with a childlike mentality of the fear of being teased and being the odd man out. I feel like I am trying to prove to myself that I can be mature by being in a relationship. Not being in a relationship makes me feel like I just entered middle school for the first time. Both the movies and my peers have told me that not being in a relationship or at least hooking up with people by the time you are fourteen years old makes you the weird kid and an undesirable.

To put it in the most blatant terms, fuck that. I know I am not an undesirable, and I know I am worthy of love. But, I am still incredibly anxious for a relationship, which means I am probably anxious for someone to tell me these things. I am also an incredibly inpatient person, so that could be another reason I am looking a relationship right now. I want to prove to everyone that I am an adult and no longer the twelve-year-old kid that is unsure of himself and everything that he is. And, to be honest, I want someone to watch a movie with that will also hold me and eat with me because eating ice cream is not fun when done alone.

◆

I am an eighteen-year-old virgin, and that is not ok. I should either be dating multiple people by now or have at least hooked up with a quarter of my graduating class in the name of sexual freedom. But, I also know that no one actually gives a shit when it comes to how many people I have been with. Yes, I am worthy of being in a relationship. I know this, but do I really? What if I can't handle being in one? What if the idea of being in a relationship is clouding my vision of what a real relationship is like? One thing that is good about not watching porn like the other teenage lads is that I don't have a totally skewed vision of what sex is actually like by watching how the porn stars do it. Well, that's not even that true because my idea of sex is taken from yesterday's episode of your favorite soap opera or film based on a book by Nicholas Sparks, so I also have a skewed view of sex and relationships.

I am possibly entering college as a dateless virgin, which fits the criteria of what many people tell me: college is my "window" of relationships. That terrified me when I was a twelve year old and going through puberty, and that terrifies me now. Are you telling me that everything I have seen in terms of relationships will not be experienced for myself until I enter college? I am eighteen years old, but I feel like the epitome of arrested development: while I am an adult physically, I am still a young teenager emotionally and romantically.

Of course, the end of my high school career forces me to reflect on what I have done and what is still to come. I remember being a freshman in high school and thinking that a relationship would just fall on me in the most unexpected of ways because that's what happens in the movies. Now, as I look back on my high school experiences, I realize that high school relationships do not always happen the way they do in the movies. I have always realized this in some way, but I would ignore it when I would think about being able to talk to the guy that is in a different social group than me and probably does not want to be with me since he hooked up with a girl at last week's party.

Fantasizing about being in a relationship with someone is so much easier than actually trying to talk to the guy you have been fantasizing about for that period of time. There's no judging and there's no chance for humiliation because it is all in your head, and no one besides you can come up with the story that you are telling. I've fantasized about relationships when I was thirteen, and I continue to do it as an eighteen-year-old, and I have no idea when that is going to "magically" end. Does that ever end? Is there an expiration date to when we are allowed to fantasize about relationships? Besides sounding very Carrie Bradshaw of me (and I am proud of it), I feel like I have to constantly prove myself worthy of being an official "adult," and I have always assumed sex and relationships to be classified as something that is very "adult."

Although each are considered something that is "mature," we see people considered children doing it all the time. I always hear about the latest hook ups between the fourteen-year-olds, and I am horrified to compare my relationship experience with one of a "mature" young teenager. In this way, I would have to consider age just a number because it does not totally define emotional maturity. Sure, I have grown emotionally between the time I was fourteen and eighteen, but that was not only because I aged. I grew emotionally because it was the response to the experiences I have had.

Professionally, I have had some much-needed growth. Instead of always sitting around and dreaming about the kind of things I want to work on, I have started to leave my shell and start pursuing them. I also have the power to control my own hobbies and my pursuits. I am not able to control relationships, which is incredibly frustrating and horrifying at times. In that way, my relationship life has been on arrested development, which is why the "age" gap between my professional and romantic life is a few years apart, or at least in my world. In my head, I should have been in at least one long relationship with someone that loves me and does not mind me sharing my life to the public. In reality, I am a single guy that still shares his life publically.

I cannot change what has happened in the past (or, in this case, what has not happened in the past). As I think about how my life came to be where it is today, that is something I have learned. No matter how many times I have wanted to change my actions in the past, whether it was not saying that nasty comment to a friend or talking to that guy that I could have had a conversation with at least once, I have to understand and accept that I cannot change it. I remember being fourteen years old and believing that I would be in a relationship by the time I turned sixteen. I also remember telling my friends that I probably would not be in a relationship in high school and them responding with, "Don't say that! You don't know that!"

I am eighteen-years-old, and I have never been in a relationship. I have never been kissed either, which makes me a super virgin and a character in an uncomfortable romantic comedy. I am the token virgin character that would make the audience laugh with their strange and horrific tendencies that they would show on their first dates. I am also the person that would get the weird look from a group of people because I am one of the few people that has the same romantic history as a newborn baby. I am the person that used to be ashamed of being a virgin. I am the person that is still sometimes ashamed of being a virgin.

I have to remind myself that being eighteen does not mean that I have one foot in the door of death, as much as people like to believe that being eighteen is incredibly old. I also have to remind myself that being eighteen does not meant that I have to immediately have to lose my virginity because I have not "caught up with everyone else and it will be too late." Please. I am the first person to admit that I want to be in a relationship because I want someone that loves me for who I am and will sit on the couch and watch television with me and enjoy my company. I also know that relationships do not totally work like this, and the baggage that comes with it becomes larger and larger as the time spent together has grown. But, as I said before, I have the mentality of a twelve-year-old when it comes to relationships, so I am getting there as fast as I can.

I cannot change the fact that I have never been in a relationship by the time I turned eighteen. I am accepting this. All I can do at this point is move forward and remind myself that I cannot totally control how my romantic life is going to turn out in the same way that I can control what I am writing down on the page. Life just does not work like that, as I have come to realize. Being eighteen does not mean that I have to meet a certain level of romantic experience, or else there would not be people experience love for the first time in their twenties or thirties. But, there are many times I have not put this into perspective, and I get lost in my own insecurities and shame when I really have nothing to be shameful for. Not being in a relationship does not discredit my accomplishments nor define who I am as a forming adult.

Romantically, my growth is stunted, but I am able to connect it with my eighteen year old "wisdom" and come up with this conclusion: the world is most definitely not ending because I am an eighteen-year-old virgin for two reasons:

1. Because no one cares about this other than myself.
2. Because I have so many more exciting things going on in my life that will keep me crazy and sane at the same time.

As someone in a cheesy musical would say to me, my time is coming, and then my time will probably come again because the first relationship will probably not work out, and then my time will probably come again four more times until I get married. Even after that, my time might come again because the divorce rate is over 50% and hideous, so who knows. What I do know now is this: I am an eighteen-year-old virgin, and things will be just fine.

"You Cannot Be Replaced"

Ode to All of the Awkward Assemblies

Assemblies are usually double-edges swords, and we all know it. We are able to get out of class, which is always exciting and welcome in my book (especially during any science or math class). But, we have to sit down and listen to grown adults tell us how much we matter, even though most of them have not had a "1" in front of their age in twenty to thirty years. Two parents that lived about an hour away from me hosted the last assembly I attended. In their town, multiple teenagers committed suicide, and they now go to different schools to talk to students about how they can "not be replaced."

While this is a message that is not totally new to me, as many strangers come in and talk to students as if we are all ready to commit suicide before they spread their magic words on us, it was the first time I really started to think about what those words really meant.

You cannot be replaced.

No one can replace you.

To be replaced in the first place, I would have had to been someone. I would have had to been someone that make a mark in the world, or at least among the student body. I would have had to do something that becomes my "trademark" with the other students.

Here is the problem with a message that pertains to not being able to be replaced: people tell us this during a time when we do not know who the hell we even are. Why is a stranger telling me that I cannot be replaced when they do not even know me? That's a little ironic to me. A stranger is telling me that I cannot be replaced in the world when they do not even know what my mine is.

I don't know if it is a situation that is easier said than done. It seems to be easy to tell a room full of unsure teenagers that there is only one of them in the world and no one can ever replace them. But, what about everything we learn about college admissions? We strive to show off how "different" we are because we are reminded that there are so many people that are the "same" as us and colleges have no reason to admit us over someone else because we are practically the "same." So yes, it might be easier to tell students that they cannot be replaced than actually having students feel like they cannot be replaced. I think teenagers live in a world full of contradicting statements and behaviors, created by both other teenagers and grown adults, and it leads them to be confused about who they are "supposed" to be and the world they are "running" one day, as we are always told.

◆

A few weeks before I started writing this essay, I received a phone call from a friend late at night. It is typical for us to speak at an ungodly hour, so it was not surprising that we were talking this late, But, that night became one that I would never forget, and the words that were said linger over me like the memories of the years I was chubby that are now contained in hideous photographs.

She began talking about the idea of being passionate about something, and it was not the first time we discussed passions. I have learned that senior year forces you to think about what your passions are and what you have been doing to follow them. Basically, senior year makes you questions what the fuck you have done for the past four years. Some memories make you feel proud of yourself because you have made the strides into becoming who you are today, and some make you feel terrible because it has made you become who you are today (re. the double edge sword mentioned before).

My friend joined our school's theatre program during our freshman year in high school. I did not do many clubs during my freshman year, if I remember correctly. Actually, I only remember really doing the school newspaper that year, and that was partially because I had to write articles for the journalism class I was taking. I was nervous to join clubs, and I had no idea what I really wanted to do. I was also struggling with accepting myself after coming out to my friends and my family a few months earlier, so I spent the year trying to "find myself" and actually like myself for who I am. Basically, that means I spent the year crying my eyes out because I wanted to change what I could not change. So, joining the theatre program was not entirely in the cards for me.

I eventually joined the theatre program during my sophomore year per my friend's suggestion (practical force). I was put into the ensemble for the fall drama, which was totally fine with me because I have never acted before and it allowed me to work with other ensemble members for the few moments I had in the show. The show went well, and I genuinely enjoyed acting in it. I did not know if theatre was for me entirely, but I was willing to give it a shot. I met a lot of people that first year that I call my friends today, but there was a group that was formed during our freshman year, which included my friend that brought me in to the program, and it was initially hard for me to connect with them since they were already an established group. Besides that, the people in that specific group were very passionate and excited about theatre, and I was not entirely in that boat because I did not know if theatre was for me.

When the spring musical began, I immediately knew that I would not enjoy performing because I was horrified at the thought of singing and dancing in front of an audience. I always thought I looked like a giant horse being killed when I sing and dance, so I did not have high hopes for myself when I thought about performing on stage. Instead, I decided to join the stage management team (at the time, the team was one person) and become the assistant stage manager for the show. I was the assistant stage manager for the rest of sophomore year and the beginning of junior year with the fall drama, and then I moved to house managing for the spring musical for junior year. By the time senior year rolled around, I went back to acting in the fall drama and then worked on the public relations team (again, a team of only one person) for my final spring musical.

When I received the phone call from my friend, it was the last week of the senior year spring musical. Truthfully, I was both sad and excited about the show ending. I was ready to move on from the theatre program, even though I was not sure what I was going to do. I just knew that I was not as passionate about theatre as many of the other students were, and I was personally ready for my time there to be over.

On the other hand, my friend was incredibly passionate about theatre, and she was grieving the end of it more than I did, which was totally understandable. I wished I were more passionate about theatre so I could share the same feelings everyone else had about the end. Of course, I was sad about leaving the program because I became so used to being there with the same people every day. But, I was never able to call it a second home to me. Not in the same way everyone else seemed to feel about it. The theater was not a second home to me. It just became a place I became used to being in and a place where I could hang out with my friends while a show was produced by the end of a few months.

That is why the phone call was so brutal for me. My friend told me that she was worried that my only identity was being the "gay kid" and she did not want that to be my only identity. The phone call led to her having me question my passions and resulted in me bawling my eyes out once I put the phone down. I was hurt because it felt like my friend shot me in the face with her own gun and then tried to heal me. I was hurt because she told me one of my greatest fears to my face. I was hurt because she was brutally honest. I was hurt because I felt that she was saying it out of care and was not meant to be malicious. I was hurt because she was right in a way, and I knew it.

I was part of the theatre program for the majority of my high school career, and I have never felt passionate about it. I never felt like I totally fit in there, despite having friends there, but I always insisted on coming back even during times when I questioned what my place would be there. I did not realize how fast the time really goes by. I remember talking to a senior when I was sophomore about my time in high school. She said it would go by so quickly, but she was totally done with the theatre program. I remember agreeing with her, and I was only a sophomore that was finishing my first year in the program. Before I knew it, I became a senior that felt the same way about this place since he walked into the theater the first time. And before I knew it, my time there was over.

I have always tried to find my identity, and I have always tried to find the reason why I "should not be replaced," but sometimes living in fantasy is easier than dealing with reality. I am definitely the first person to admit that I live in my head a lot. I consider myself someone that is social and able to connect with people easily, but I am also someone that is able to stay in my head for a while and just imagine different aspects of my life and how it could be. Imagining talking to a guy is easier than actually talking to the guy. Thinking about what I would write in this essay is easier than actually sitting down and writing the damn essay.

Once my friend told me that she was nervous that my only identity would be being the "gay kid," I cried because I felt that I "wasted" so much time, even though I know I didn't totally do that.

What the fuck? How the hell did I get here?

In a way, I felt like an addict that just woke up from a bad binge. Confused and disoriented. I did not need to do something extreme, like a drug binge, to feel completely disoriented and uncomfortable. Rather, just living my life and reflecting on it after did the job. All I was doing was living my life without totally thinking about all of the choices I was making. Do I regret participating in the theatre program? Absolutely not. Not only did I make great friends there, but I also learned a lot through each job that I had there. For someone that did not totally feel like I fit in with the "theatre crowd," I really was the program whore. I literally did everything except build the sets, and there was a time where I thought about doing that. Granted, it was a very small period of time because I soon realized that giving me a power tool is equivalent to giving a overzealous first grader a power tool, so I knew that was not going to work out well.

Besides that, I learned a lot of important things throughout my time in the theatre program that I would not have learned if I chose to not join any clubs and go home and cry while eating chocolate every day. Still, my friend's words rang true to me because I did not really have a passion in theatre that lent itself to a identity for me there. I was not the "actor" or the "dancer" or the "costumer." Instead, I was the person that ran around and did multiple jobs in his time there. In more positive terms, I have heard that I am just "Brandon" or the "funny" guy. Doing stand-up has lent itself to me having the "funny" title or just the "honest" description because I do not go on stage with a script and pretend to be a character. Instead, I walk on stage and talk about my own life and stories from it. In the theatre program, I had nothing really to call myself.

After the phone call ended, I took the time during the late hours of the night (where many of the best ideas come into fruition) to think about my next step. I knew I could sit there and cry about what my friend said to me. Or I could cry because I thought about what the hell I did for all of high school. But, I knew I could not get that time back no matter how long I cried about it. High school was ending soon, and there would never be an opportunity to change what I chose to do when I was fourteen and fifteen years old. That just cannot happen, no matter how much I have wanted things to change. Instead, I knew I would have to more forward and decide which steps to take moving on.

Basically, my goal became how to make myself "someone that cannot be replaced." How the hell does one make themselves not able to be replaced? To this day, I am not sure because there is not a set answer. It seems that it is just what each person makes of it. As long as someone feels they cannot be replaced, that is just how it is. When I was on the phone, I realized that I did not totally feel that way about myself. But, I knew what some of my passions were, and no one could take that away from me. I am passionate about making people laugh and being able to connect with my own experiences. I am passionate about being relatable to people so they know that they are not alone in whatever they have been through. I am passionate about being a good friend, son, brother. I am passionate about being a good person in a world where there seems to be so much bad behavior.

Do I know exactly what I am going to do with my life? No. Do I know where I am going be five years from now? Absolutely not. Just because we want or expect something does not mean it will automatically become a reality. I have learned that when I realize that I am still single and not a famous comedian at the age of eighteen. Some learn this when they do not get accepted into their dream college. Others learn this when they do not get to eat what they want for dinner.

I am still learning what it means to not be able to be replaced. Yes, we are told this all the time. But, I think we can understand that there is a difference between being the person that is out there and changing the world with whatever we choose to do and being the person that sits on the couch and chooses to do absolutely nothing in the name of laziness. This is coming from a upper-middle class suburban kid, and I am so lucky to be able to come from a family and an area that pushes people to be successful. I also realize that there in the same world, there are many people that do not have the opportunity to be successful and thrive because they are struggling to survive. Or, they are struggling to keep their family afloat, and they are doing what they can to stay alive. I also know that there are people who are told every day they are replaceable and there so many others like them that can do what they are passionate about, but they can "do it better." I know there are people out there that are told they are worth nothing and can do nothing because they are a failure and someone who do not deserve to be successful.

Here's one thing I know: in the very lucky position that I am in, I can either sit back and do nothing or I can be the person that helps change the views of others. I can be part of the world that allows everyone to succeed, no matter where you come from. I want to be someone that helps others and tries to make a change because I realize that so many people have not had the same childhood and upbringing as I had. I want to be someone that cannot actually be replaced.

I want to assume that this is one of the underlying messages that each person from each assembly has told students. Unfortunately, I was too ignorant to really think about it most of the time. But, I am choosing to think about it now. I see what those speakers were trying to do. They are talking to the ones that have the opportunity to make the change, as long as there is someone there that is listening.

I know I will not be just the "gay kid" because, although being gay is absolutely part of who I am (and I am always proud to identify as such), it is not all who I am. And for the first time, I am thinking about how I can be someone that cannot be replaced, and I think I am getting there.

Why I Hate Urinals

I have always said urinals are made by the devil, and I am standing by that statement. Even as an atheist, I can even understand that the maker of the urinal has a bit of the devil in them. If you cannot tell, I am not a supporter of the urinal. One has probably said that the urinal is a great way for men to be able to pee without having to use a full-on toilet. Urinals are quick, and they are suited well for men and their package. I have seen many men confidently pee in their urinal like they own it, and I am the person that is constantly trying to make sure that no one can see my area instead of peeing comfortably.

You know how teachers usually have their own bathrooms in school? I really hope I do not sound like a upper-middle class asshole by saying that, because I am going to assume that every school has at least one faculty bathroom where students are not allowed to enter or else they are shot by the hall monitor (Truth: I have never seen an actual hall monitor in my life, so I am going to assume they just do not exist at all). For me, using the bathroom in school is already a slightly uncomfortable experience. It's not like I have ever had a really bad and embarrassing toilet story that has happened in the school. Thank GOODNESS! That's actually one of my worst nightmares. But, I will never forget the epic nosebleed I had my sophomore year. I was sitting in English class and trying to write an overly-dramatic piece about an a married couple when my nose just started randomly bleeding everywhere and it left a trail on the ground as I walked to the bathroom in shame. It looked like an episode of any shitty crime show because it resulted in me sitting on the toilet seat with blood everywhere because standing for fifteen minutes with a bloody nose got tiring.

So, the bathroom is not my favorite place to be in the school. Besides that story, I also always happen to be in the bathroom at the same time someone is relieving themselves from apparently the worst lunch they have ever had in their life, according to the smell. Which, by the way, always leads me to feel bad for those people. I mean, imagine not having the choice of using the bathroom or not because someone is so sick they either have to use the bathroom or relieve themselves in their pants, which is just plain horrific at any age past baby years.

But, even though walking in on this kind of a situation is most definitely not pleasant (as if I am the one that is suffering through that when it is actually just me being an asshole), the worst kind of bathroom interaction is when a teacher walks in and decides to use the urinal right next to the one you have decided to get comfortable with for thirty seconds.

Usually when a teacher decides to use the urinal next to mine, my first thought is to run out the door before I can even get my pants buttoned. But, since I have to act somewhat adult-like, my only option is to stay and continue the process as one of the people I moan about the most to my friends and strangers is urinating right next to me. Since I also treat teachers as if they were celebrities and had absolutely no lives outside of the classroom, I always get very wound up and nervous whenever I see a teacher outside of the classroom and outside of school. So, to have a teacher peeing next to me is equivalent to having one of the members of One Direction peeing right next to me.

Now, this is why urinals have become the devil. For some reason, lots of men think that urinals are the new hangout place and/or place to have a nice lovely daily discussion. I do not get this craze where it is not suddenly alright to have a discussion with someone who is next to you in the urinal. I mean, I guess that is alright when you are with your friends because I've had chats with some of my friends while they are using the bathroom, but I am talking about one of those situations where you are only talking to an acquaintance or, even worse, a teacher that just graded a test you know you bombed two periods before.

Here is an example of a conversation I once had with a teacher while using the bathroom.

I am quietly peeing when Mr. JustGaveUsAHardTest walks in and chooses to pee in the urinal right next to mine.

Mr. JGUAHT: Hey there, Brandon!

Me: Hello…

Mr. JGUAHT: How's it going?

(At this point, I already want to run out of the bathroom faster than a bat out of hell).

Me: Fine, thanks. How about you?

Mr. JGUAHT: It's going alright.

At this point, which might be worse than actually just having a conversation, we are both silently peeing while trying to look away from each other.

Mr. JGUAHT chooses to shake his ding-dong at this point to season some more liquid awkwardness into the urinal.

Mr. JGUAHT: Well, see you in class!

Me: Bye!

In the course of my high school career, I have also walked into bathrooms and find a teacher already invading the urinal, and I immediately walk out of the bathroom before they have a chance to notice who is in the bathroom.

Those moments are always fun, and they make the best of school days even better.

◆

Since I briefly mentioned previously about the way some guys assault the urinal with their urine, I will list some of the ways I have seen guys decide to attack the throne, which I believe tells me a lot about their personality.

1. **The over-confident alpha urine-ator**

    These are the people that decide it is totally appropriate to pee by holding their junk and leaning backwards like they are in their own bathrooms. These people usually fall into the habit of standing far from the urinal to the point where the people around them can see their shlong hanging out for the world to "admire" (in their minds). I tend to associate these people with ones that think they have a shlong the size of a large candy bar when it is really the size of an over-used short pencil. No one appreciates when they throw their candy bar for everyone to see because they are usually the ones that do not have one that is worth looking at. Just saying.

2. **The shy pee-ers**

    These are the ones that pee in the urinal as if the urinal is about to attack them if they do not pee in the right spot. Some may also pee as if everyone they were peeing in front of an entire

audience and they had to cover up their junk
before a paparazzo takes a picture of it and
publishes it in a magazine. Using the bathroom
is the time where one should not have anxiety,
and I am sometimes am guilty of falling in this
category of pee-er. I tend to associate this
person with a shy person that may/may not have
had their junk exposed by accident when they
were a child and have been scarred ever since.
This happened to me once at a water park,
where I lost my pants when riding the
simulation waves and my seven-year-old junk
was out for the world to judge and laugh at it.
As you can probably tell, I am still not over this.

3. **The person that has no time to pee**
   This is the person that runs to the bathroom and
   pees as if he has no time in the world to use the
   bathroom because he is just "so busy." Please.
   That is the person that acts like he does not have
   any time to wait in the line like the rest of the
   civilians that also have to use the bathroom.
   This is the person that cuts the line in
   bathrooms, coffee places, and school carpools
   because he is too important for everyone else.
   The joke is on him because this is also the
   person that usually pees on himself a little
   because he is rushing and then pretend it was
   just a water stain from the sink after "splashing

170

water on himself." Mhmmmm. I know your tricks.

4. **The social media urine-ator**

This is the person that decides that peeing is the perfect time to check every social media they have. For some, they may check their online newspaper to see if there was any important events that happened between the time they checked their phone two minutes before to the time they took a bathroom break. Usually, nothing has happened. But, they cannot help themselves. This is also associated with the type of person that accidentally pees on himself, but that's because they did not pay attention to what they were doing because they were reminding themselves that absolutely nothing they would be interested in happened in two minutes.

So, as you can see, I am not a fan of the use of urinals and what happens while people use them. It is indeed a weird thing to hate, and I recognize that I am probably the most ridiculous person in the world. Fine. You win, world. But, I doubt anyone appreciates talking to a teacher while using the bathroom. I do not even think the most over-zealous creepy student would like to use the bathroom with their teacher next to them.

I think it is safe to say that one of my greatest fears in this cruel world is having to pee next to my boss, and I assume that would happen if the world is getting back at me for saying that one of my colleague's outfits was ugly or for not telling my co-worker that her shirt was tucked into her underwear.

As a child, I was always told to become comfortable with the uncomfortable because that is what "adults have to do." But, I do not know if I can handle this horrific ordeal. I also know that I cannot hold in my pee forever because someone I know has the possibility of being right next to me. All I am saying is that I hope the person next to me is not one of the people that I disliked in high school because the worst thing in the world is accidentally peeing on yourself while trying to joke around saying you are so excited to see the person that you just peed yourself a little. That would just be the worst, and I am pretty sure they would not find that charming at all.

The Tale of the Broken Phone

How My Phone Has Survived Everything and Then Abruptly Broke

Let's just put something on the table right away: I have had two iPhones and a Blackberry between the time I was thirteen to the time I was eighteen. Yes, you have every right to hate me. I totally understand. I would hate me as well. By the way, I had the Blackberry before I had the iPhone, so I had the Blackberry at thirteen years old. What the hell was I going to do with a Blackberry at thirteen years old? It was not like I had any important business meetings to attend to. The most important "meeting" I had during the day was my math class, and I was not even studying algebra yet.

Once I entered high school, my parents gave me my first iPhone to mark the stamp of spoiled suburban boy. I did not recognize this at the time, as I was just excited to be part of the progressing technological universe. Oh, and I was excited because my iPod could also be my phone, and that is an amazing achievement, as I am sure the creators of the iPhone were extremely excited to create a phone where young teenagers can play Angry Birds and send nude photos through Snapchat.

My phone has survived way too much, and I am surprised that my phone has stuck by me for so long. In terms of friendship, I was a terrible friend to my phone. We tend to look at phones as our children, no matter how much we do not want to admit it, and that was true for me when I first got the phone. But, over time, the novelty wore off and it became just another thing I carried with me when I hung out with my friends. The phone was the device used for my parents to get in contact with me when I went to the movie theater with my friends and they were worried we could get kidnapped in suburban New Jersey. It was also the device where I learned my favorite band was coming out with a new album. It was also the device where I learned what my friends were doing down to where they were taking a shit since it is the hub of social media.

If I had to compare my phone and myself to parents and their children, I would say that I am either the parent that does not care about their kids at all and smokes crack all day in the living room or I am the overly-annoying and scary parent/coach that will put my kid through physical pain in the name of sports and then scream at them to get over it and get up when they basically have a broken arm. I know those are two extreme kinds of parents, but stay with me here.

Everything starts off nice and innocent when you first get your new phone and take it out of the box. You vow to take care of it because it is all fresh and shiny and new, as maybe a parent would act when they first have their child. Then, before you know it, you drop your phone on the ground for the first time because the brownie, the milkshake, and the phone could not all fit in two hands when walking to the couch. Innocent enough. Fine. Luckily, there is a cute phone case that will protect your phone in the worst of situations, except for water. Don't drop it in the ocean. But, I will say, if your first thought when you jump in the pool or enter the ocean is to take a cute selfie, the phone should be falling into the water. There are no if, ands, or iPhones about it. You're done.

Ok, so your phone fell to the ground, and it has survived. Now, you are feeling a little more comfortable with your phone and the edge has been taken off a bit. Since the baby has clothes on *per se*, everything is just dandy. A few months later, you drop your phone a second time, but this time you drop it in water. If you are not terrified, I do not know what the hell is wrong with you. I know it is "just a phone," but I think we can all agree that a good portion of our lives is either spent on the phone or just saved on the phone itself. And now that is all in water.

This is where the crack-smoking parent comes in. My phone fell into the sink full of water because I chose to put it on top of a couple of small boxes and it completely slid into the water-filled sink while I was washing my face. That is like a deadbeat dad taking his kid to the park and breaking his ass bad. I looked away for two seconds and before I knew it my phone was underwater and drowning. I quickly snatch it up and try to pretend that it did not just take a bath and it was completely fine. In reality, my phone needed to go to the iHospital immediately, and I rush downstairs to throw it in a bowl of rice to dry. Because I am a moron and do not know how to survive in life with the little things, the idea to throw it in rice was the result of a five minute Internet search.

Now, this is where the crazy parent/coach comes into play. I sit down for twenty minutes and wait for my phone to start "magically" working again. Meanwhile, it is in the back of my head that my phone could be completely broken because it fell into a pool of water. It was not like my phone just suddenly stopped working and it was an interior malfunction. What would I have said to the crazy iPeople that work at the Apple store?

"Hi, I was being reckless while washing my face and my phone fell in a pool of water and now it is not working. That is completely ridiculous and it should be working at all times no matter what." I doubt the iPeople would take my complaint seriously. Besides, I am sure they are trained to find any single reason why the phone being broken was my fault, even if it was not (it so was in this situation) just so they would make you pay for the broken phone. Apparently, I was having none of that, as I mentally started yelling at the phone to be fine.

"Get up and suck it up!" My brain was channeling to the phone with absolutely no response.

Eventually, my phone was revived with success, and I continued along my merry way with my phone as if nothing happened.

Sooner or later, something happened. In my usual way, I lose track of the phone because I am carrying other important items (ie. Potato chips, my computer, my glass of water, my dignity) and I dropped my phone on the floor multiple times and it somehow survived each single time. At some point, my phone case broke and I had to remove it from my phone. Now, my phone is naked and afraid, and I was the horrible parent that did not cover it with any type of phone case at all. For teenagers, this is huge disaster, as phone cases have become a fashion trend in the world of self-indulgence and the use of parents' credit cards. I was the owner that allowed my phone to be vulnerable to the world of pavement and chewed gum.

I enter New York City on a cold winter day, and I expect it to be a calm day with a friend. I am walking with my naked phone and my wallet. Soon, I trip on absolutely nothing (one might call that air) and my phone calls face first on the ground. I pick it up, and I see that my phone, the phone I had for over two years, has smashed and shattered on the ground. It was quite a moment. I comforted myself with the shards of glass that came out of the phone, and I had to continue walking with my friend because the iHospital would not have been able to fix that situation. My phone was iShattered, and it was because I kept it naked and cold in an unforgiving and cruel world.

I would like to think my phone has the same traits as me. I tend to bottle up my emotions and be resilient until I eventually explode, and I have realized that I most definitely have to take classes on how to take care of my phone properly and respectfully. How am I supposed to take care of a dog or an actual child if I cannot even take care of a cell phone without letting it fall apart? I probably should hate myself for even saying this because this is what our generation has come to. We now treat phones like children because our entire lives are basically in it. I am that person that will tell people "a phone is just a phone" until I do not have it anymore and I feel naked because it is not in my pocket. So basically, I am the worst kind of person and I will own it. But, don't tell my phone that. I do not want it to think I am a bad owner.

Gaining a Voice

The Start of My Internship

I always thought that having an internship makes
you feel very "adult" because nothing screams adult more
than running around getting coffee for other people and
getting a payment in the form of, "This coffee does not
have enough sugar in it." Fine. That is more of my
interpretation of an intern/assistant for a really cutthroat
company where the egos are too big and the personalities
are too tight. I understand that an internship is a place for
interns to learn more about what they want to pursue in a
more hands-on approach, and I always thought that was the
coolest thing.

◆

I was raised in suburban New Jersey, and I lived
only thirty minutes outside of New York City. Despite the

distance between the two places, I have always view New York as its own world that I wanted to immerse myself in. I found the culture and the diversity in the city so electrifying and exciting, and I have loved the energy there ever since my parents took my siblings and I there for the first time.

In my town, the residents make up a cupcake that consists of white people being the actual cupcake with an Asian frosting with Hispanic sprinkles and a Black cherry on the top of it. Basically, that is my way of describing the amount of people that live in our town. It is definitely not the most diverse place, as I have come to realize. Being a White Hispanic (my father is Colombian and my mother is Irish and English), I have come to recognize this when one of my classmates told me that I am "Spanish, but not REALLY Spanish." To this day, I am not quite sure that means exactly. Another classmate asked me how I was "so tan during the winter," and I have to explain to her that it was just my normal skin color. She looked at me like I was the Hispanic Casper the Friendly Ghost.

When I became a junior in high school, my mother presented me with an exciting opportunity. She is an attorney, and one of the people that works in her office is also a Broadway producer that was starting a new company that reviews Broadway and Off-Broadway shows. He was looking for interns that could go see shows and write reviews for his website. I thought it was a great idea, but I was nervous for two reasons. 1. I was not a huge theater fan. I mean, I always enjoyed seeing shows and I always looked forward to seeing shows with my family, but I would never call myself a "theater expert." 2. I did not get this internship by myself. It was not like the producer read my writing and picked me out of a group of applicants. My mother got me the internship. It would have been silly of me not to take it, but I also knew that this was not an internship earned from hard work, and that made me feel guilty.

Despite my fears, I knew that it was a great opportunity to improve my writing and be able to see some great shows in the process. So, I took the internship and did not tell many people in theater other than my close friends in fear that they would come to my house and slaughter me. Sometimes, good news should be kept in secret, and this was one of those moments. I also knew that I had to prove myself with my writing. I was in the door as someone was holding it open for me, but I would only be able to stay in the room if my writing was on par with what they wanted and I did not hand an actual piece of dog feces with my name on it.

With this internship, I was also receiving more independence then I ever felt before. Just to be clear, my parents were never the type to keep me in the house all the time and refused to allow me to go outside and explore my surroundings. I was able to go the city with my friends a little before I turned sixteen years old, but this was different. I was going there for a purpose that was not to just have a fun day with my friends outside of our small town. I was "commuting" for a "work" related assignment. I had my notebook and a pen with me that was ready to go, and I was excited to be someone that was "official" in one of these shows. Of course, I thought I could keep my cool and composure because I was such an "adult" now. That fantasy was shattered like my broken phone (and my dignity) when I entered the box office for my first show and they had no idea who I was or why I was coming to the show. As in, they did not have my name on any list and they were asking me if the tickets were under someone else's name. At this point, I was sweating like a criminal in court because I was with my best friend and I no longer looked like an official "important person." Oh, the joys of being seventeen. So young. So much to learn. Before you get your panties in a bunch, I know that I am eighteen and a moron.

I eventually get the tickets, and the show was a wonderful experience. Once it was over, the actors' and crew's families were waiting outside for the talent to visit them. My friend ran off to the bathroom to pee out her $7 soda, and I waited on the couch and watched as everyone was greeting each other. I reviewed the show before it opened, and the families were the ones that seemed to fill the seats of the preview shows since it was a small Off-Broadway show in a small theatre. Nevertheless, I was starstruck by the performers and felt like the little kid that had no where to sit at the lunch tables at school because everyone's families were together while my friend and I were the equivalent to Romy and Michele at their high school reunion.

Throughout the course of a few months, I was able to see a few more shows both by myself and with friends and reviewed them the next day. I loved being able to go to the city and enter the smell theatres with my "official" reviewer title. It was both amazing to see the talent and the audience because I was reminded of the diversity that truly exists that I do not get to always see back home. Since I spent most of my life in one town, I have felt like it is the place where I will be forever, much to my disdain. It's not because I do not like the town or the people in it. It is because there is so much more I want to see and experience before I settle down in one place for what would seem to be the rest of my life.

Being in high school, I have become guilty of sometimes acting like high school is what controls your life and the only thing that matters is doing well there so you can get into a "great" college. I sometimes forget that there is so much more outside of my high school and outside of my small town because I get so consumed in, frankly, the bullshit of it all. I get crazy about grades and doing the best I can in classes when, at the end of the day, how I do on one test is not going to control how my entire life is going to be.

We are reminded so much that every move we make as students will affect which school we get into and how well we will do in school and how the rest of our lives is going to be. It is overwhelming and scary to think about what your life is going to be life when you are only fifteen years old. At times, it feels like a drive by shooting when an adult gives you all of these warnings about how "terrible" our lives could be if do not make the right decisions and then they end it with a "good luck!" note to cover up the wound they just gave us.

Watching the performers on stage, I starting thinking about all the things adults have told us since were children. We are told to fit in and do things that fit the "mold" of being "good children," and then we are told to make ourselves stand out so we can look appealing to colleges. At the end of the day, we are all just trying to make it. We all have moments where we begin playing characters of ourselves. Who am I as a human being? I am not the guy who makes funny jokes who writes a lot and acts respectful to people all the time. Yes, that is what colleges see me as because that is how I have presented myself to them. Hell, that is how I present myself to many new people I meet. But, that is not always me.

My name is Brandon Alvarado. I like to make jokes to people and I love writing. I try to be respectful as I can be to everyone. I am someone that cries when I am upset, and I have been guilty of being overly emotional and wearing my heart on my sleeve. I laugh really hard when I find something funny, and I even laugh at jokes that are off-hand and inappropriate. I love being able to laugh because it reminds me that the world is not always full of stress. I love to eat a lot of food when I am hungry, happy, sad, or bored. I love my friends and family, but I sometimes do not speak up when I feel sad or hurt even though I know

I should say something. And I am not a perfect human being. I am not a performer. I am just me.

Living in a small town allows me to really see one slice of life, even though I know it is not accurate of the world. With my internship, I have been able to see different parts of life with different kinds of people come together to support something that we all care about. And, it has allowed me to learn that there is so much more to see and understand that just what is immediately next to my house. There is a world that I do not know entirely about yet, but I am excited to be able to go out and see it with clearer eyes.

I am not a perfect person, and I never will be. All I can do is try and understand the parts of the life that I do not understand. I can only try to be open to all kinds of people and all kinds of life, and I can try and change the world one step at a time. I am learning to finally gain a voice and to be able to speak so someone else can do the same thing I am trying to do: to understand the world they do not see themselves every day. To have their own voice.

I saw my first article with my name on it a few weeks after I saw my first show, and I smiled at the thought of writing something for someone to read, even if it was a review for a show that someone might want to see. I know it will not be the last time I see my name under an article, whether it is through another review or this essay. I know I will get there, and I am excited to gain my voice.

The Ali Effect

I was in the local toy store with my oversized outfit and fourth grade attitude when I bought my first journal. It was a *High School Musical* themed journal with Zac Efron, who was sporting an early 2000s bowl cut that we pretended was acceptable because it was Zac Efron, and Vanessa Hudgens, who was known as Vanessa Anne Hudgens at the time because it was the pre-nude photo scandal that made Disney executives angry after definitely staring at them for more than two hours first.

I hurried home with my new journal with the intent of writing everything from what I was eating for dinner that night to what I was secretly going to eat later when my parents weren't looking to my dreams of becoming a superstar. I would try to write in the journal every day because I became obsessed with the idea of having someone finding my journal when I died so they could read my latest post about the success of the Alvarado Christmas 2007.

I don't remember the exact moment I started writing about Ali, who was a fictional character I created in my writings, but I do remember how she truly took over my writings the way a muse would (if a fourth grader could have a muse). She didn't have much depth to her when she was first created. She had blonde hair and blue eyes, and she was very smart. She had the perfect body, and she was the most confident person you can imagine. While it started off as something that was fun to write about, Ali was a character that was developed more thoroughly when I was in middle school. She was no longer just the perfect person without a story. Instead, she struggled with adversity, as she was adopted after living with a single addict mother. She overcame her adversity by working hard in school and also managing to have her own television show. She had the girl next door look that made her look like one of those child models you can find on Twitter if you want to feel bad about yourself, and she was always willing to both shop and play any sport you can possibly offer her. All the boys fell in love with her instantly, but she already had a steady boyfriend at the ripe age of 12.

I really didn't make the connection between Ali and my own insecurities until I look back on my own behavior at that time. It was a release for me to be able to write about Ali and her experiences. I wouldn't even write stories about her most of the time. Usually, I would write little things that made her grow as a character, and I would just keep adding details to her overall story. I thought I was happy when I would sit down to write about her life, but I didn't realize at the time how unhappy I was. Ali had the life I wanted to live in many ways. I was fully aware that I would never be able to live the life I created in my own mind, and that is what drew me to keep writing about Ali. Though I knew I would never live the life that "she" had, there was always something comforting about being able to create this character and this new world. At the same time, I didn't know that creating this world was holding me back from becoming comfortable with myself in the real world.

It was the end of the torturous middle school years when a friend discovered my Ali writings. Luckily for myself, my fourth grade journal was filled with fourth grade nonsense, and I moved my writings over to an equally embarrassing *Twilight* journal I bought at the local Barnes and Noble. Some of the writings were also moved to white printer paper (because that is what it truly means to live a professional lifestyle). My friend and I were gearing up to watch the Emmy Award winning and thought-provoking drama, *Jersey Shore*, when she saw the writings hanging from my bedroom drawer. After asking who Ali was, I quickly took the papers, shoved them back into the drawer, and my friend and I pretended the situation didn't just happen as we were taken into the tropical world of Seaside Heights, New Jersey. While that day made me think about how watching *Jersey Shore* was fifty shades of wrong, it also forced me to think about the role Ali, a fictional character, played in my life. Having my friend find my writings made me feel like my pants were quickly pulled down in front of an audience, and I didn't know what the right things to say was. I also didn't know what to think of myself, but that changed as I grew older.

After that day, I began to try and change the way I viewed myself, as cliché as that sounds. Ali consumed my life to the point where I sometimes thought about how she would react to the everyday occurrences in my real life. She became an extension of me in the worst ways. I no longer knew how to control her in my own mind, but I knew where I could start. Ali came into my life when I had no confidence in myself, and she stayed with me as I went from liking myself a little bit to completely hating myself to slowly beginning to like myself again. I knew I couldn't get Ali out of my life until I began truly loving myself for all that I am. I didn't let go of Ali the day my friend discovered her, but I slowly grew to love myself more than I loved the idea of Ali. From there, I began throwing my writings relating to Ali in the garbage. I threw away all of the printer pages that were filled with the writings, and I threw away the *Twilight* journal because it was completely unnecessary, whether it had writings relating to Ali or not. Once the writings were gone, I began to let go of Ali from my mind. I no longer wanted Ali to be the extension of me, or the person that I always wished I could be. Over time, I no longer wanted to be like Ali, as I recognized all of the good qualities in myself that lead me to want to be me.

After Ali was gone from my life, I bought a new blank journal with a black cover. I opened it up and decided what to write. While Ali was out of my life, there was someone else I wanted to write about. I took the pen, and I started jotting down the feelings of someone that was not an extension of me. I let go of that person before, and she took the insecurity and fear with her. Instead, I started writing about Brandon.

Acknowledgements

I cannot believe that I wrote my first my first book!
I hope it is the first of many because I truly enjoyed writing
every essay. This book should have taken many months to
write, and somehow it was finished in three months. So, if
there was a typo, sorry... But you can't get your money
back. But I'm sure the pages will make for a great fire, if
you choose to get your money's worth after you finishing
reading it.

I have many people to thank for their contributions
to the book and keeping my sanity, so let's begin...

Mr. Rawson, you have worn a couple of hats during
this process, as you were both my senior project mentor
and the editor for this book. Thank you so much for
everything you have done to help the book come together
and helping me create this project that I will always be
proud of. Without you, this project could not have and
would not have happened, and I am sure I have said this to
you in multiple emails, But, it cannot be said enough.
Thank you.

My parents and my siblings, who are the people that
have never seen a word of any of the essays in this book,

are probably horrified by some of what they have read. I basically kept the book as a surprise to all of you, so thank you for always being supportive of my endeavors, as a project like this can either make a parent proud or totally embarrass them. I hope you are not embarrassed, and I hope that I was right when I promised that I only wrote nice things about all of you. I kind of forgot some of what I wrote, so let's hope for the best!

Tyler, you were the only friend I named in the book, and I did not actually do that on purpose, but I have to thank you for being my friend through thick and thin. You also did not read any of the essays until now, as I really haven't shown anyone besides Mr. Rawson any of the essays before I actually released the book. We have certainly been on a ride together since we became friends, and I would not have had it any other way. No matter what, you are literally my right arm, which some people might find weird. But, that's ok. I love you. Always.

To all of my other friends, who are absolutely not playing second fiddle to Tyler but just aren't named in this book, thank you for all of your support and love throughout this process. All of my friends know that I need people to tell me a thousand times to do something before I actually feel confident enough to do it. That is how I began doing stand-up, and that is how this book happened. Thank you all for pushing me into working on this project because I could have been sitting on the couch watching reality TV instead of writing these acknowledgements.

To all of the people that donated to my Kickstarter campaign, including Dana Shulman, Vittoria Fronte, Josh Kim, Alyssa Zoll, Gina Romana, Mrs. Dorely Leal-Drago, Mrs. Sheri Grubman, Randy Perimutter, Mrs. Valerie Mattessich, Lauren Iannotta, Jessica Kronenberger, Fia Brunou, Lisa Iannaccone- Scher, Jamie Ryu, Larry Gevirtz, Kaitlyn Lewis, Cristen Sommers, Mrs. Karen Kosch, Christine Franklin, Suzie Fiat, Jessica Nasib, Julianna Bottiglieri, Mrs. Bonnie Slockett, Elyse Elisano, Maria Hinrichsen, Mrs. Sheba Buckley, Ms. Elizabeth Egan, Mr. Bill Rawson, Tim Staines, The Toci Family, Eileen Proven, Alex Brennan, Jessie Fillare, Haley Schaumberger, and Marissa Cornejo.

Thank you to Molly Henry, who created the best cover I could have ever asked for. I am so bad at anything relating to graphic design (I can't even draw a picture well), and I literally threw my ideas to her and asked her to create it. Thank you so much for creating the look of this entire book, as it really is the first thing people see when they look at the book. It's absolutely perfect, and I am so grateful.

And finally, to all the readers that bought this book, without all of you, this book would be nothing, and you all get my eternal gratitude for helping both my self-esteem and my college funds. I cannot thank you enough for buying the book, and I'm sure it will be a great item to re-gift to the weird Uncle you forgot you had/ignore at every family gathering.